Praise for *Suicide of the West*

'. . . rare insight and analysis, and some troubling conclusions . . . The authors have sounded a wake-up call and provided a solution at one and the same time.'
(Sir Menzies Campbell, Leader of the Liberal Democrats)

'. . . describes a past of accomplishment and a present of fragility. It must point thinking people to new efforts to safeguard valued freedoms and culture . . .'
(Neil Kinnock, former Labour Leader and European Commissioner)

'You finish the book with the uncomfortable feeling that the authors are asking the right question: is the future of our values and our civilization secure?'
(Matthew Parris, columnist, *The Times*)

'This book could not be more timely.'
(John Blundell, Director General, Institute of Economic Affairs)

'. . . a salutary wake-up call to shake off fear, cynicism and depression . . . and reclaim optimism about onward human progress.'
(Polly Toynbee, writer and columnist, *The Guardian*)

'A powerful and challenging analysis of the values underlying Western society's remarkable success, and the threats to the West's survival from its equally remarkable loss of self-confidence.'
(Lord Blackwell, former Head of the PM's Policy Unit, 10 Downing Street)

'Take care. This book may change the way you think . . . a must read for leaders in politics, business, and the community.'
(Professor Andrew Campbell, Founder, Ashridge Strategic Management Centre)

'An eye-opener of a book . . . brilliant insight into where the solutions might lie.'
(Sir Stephen Sherbourne, political strategist, former adviser to Margaret Thatcher)

'. . . we seem to be making an alarmingly good effort at [the suicide of the West], as this book clearly indicates.'
(Simon Jenkins, journalist)

'An original and arresting thesis . . . a great achievement. Read it and you'll never think of our world in quite the same way.'   (Andrew Roberts, historian and author)

'An urgent and eloquent shock to the system . . .'
(Martin Kettle, columnist, *The Guardian*)

'Important, stimulating and very timely . . . places current debates within a highly illuminating historical context.'   (Lord Puttnam, film-maker)

'A wonderful book combining history, economics, business, and politics. Should be read by every aspiring leader in business and society.'
(Peter Johnson, Fellow, Exeter College, Oxford University)

Also available from Continuum:

Humanity, Terrorism, Terrorist War – Ted Honderich
The West and the Rest – Roger Scruton
The Dignity of Difference – Jonathan Sacks
Where Have All the Intellectuals Gone? – Frank Furedi

Suicide of the West

Richard Koch
and
Chris Smith

continuum
LONDON • NEW YORK

Continuum International Publishing Group
The Tower Building   80 Maiden Lane
11 York Road   Suite 704
London SE1 7NX   New York NY 10038

British Library Cataloguing-in-Publication Data
A catalogue record for this book is available from the British Library.

ISBN: 0–8264–9023–9 (hardback)

Library of Congress Cataloging-in-Publication Data
A catalog record for this book is available from the Library of Congress.

Typeset by Kenneth Burnley, Wirral, Cheshire
Printed and bound in Great Britain by MPG Books Ltd, Bodmin, Cornwall

Contents

For Lee Dempsey and Dorian Jabri

Acknowledgements

One of the pleasures of writing a book crossing several disciplines is that we have been introduced to a whole raft of books and research that was previously new to us. Sometimes this has been a matter of voracious reading and trial and error, but in many cases we were fortunate enough to be pointed in the right direction by the kindness of friends. We must say that they are too many to mention all individually – not least in case we forget anyone (it has been known) – but we would like to thank especially John Blundell, Roger Bootle, Nicholas Brealey, Andrew Campbell, David Cannadine, Chris Eyles, Rick Haller, Peter Johnson, Martin Nye, Chris Outram, Andrew Roberts, A. F. (Pat) Thompson, and George Walden for their expertise and generosity with their time.

We owe a particular debt to Robin Field, who collaborated with one of the authors on much of the research and ideas that eventually went into the chapters on Growth and Individualism. Many of the ideas in these chapters derive from Robin or from our discussions with him, and he was extremely kind to agree that they could be incorporated in this book.

The thesis on which the book was based was extensively circulated and commented upon by many excellent thinkers. We do not imply that any of them endorse our views, but they have certainly stimulated our thoughts. Again by exception we thank Marcus Alexander, Lord (Norman) Blackwell, Peter Englander, Frank Field, Richard Fuller, John Hewitt, Tony Kippenberger, John Micklethwait, Ferdinand Mount, Jesse Norman, Martin Nye, Michael Obermayer, Chris Outram, Matthew Parris, Michael Portillo,

Jamie Reeve, David J. Reynolds, Andrew Roberts, Anthony Rice, Stephen Sherbourne, and Philip Webster for their outstandingly helpful input.

A work of synthesis such as this rests directly on the work and insights of hundreds of other writers. We have drawn attention to the most important of these in our footnotes, but certain books were so seminal that we would like to highlight them and thank their authors: Manuel Castells for *The Rise of the Network Society*, Niall Ferguson for *Colossus*, Geert Hofstede for *Culture's Consequences*, Keith Hopkins for *A World Full of Gods*, Samuel P. Huntington for *The Clash of Civilizations* and *Who Are We?*, Richard E. Nisbett for *The Geography of Thought*, Steven Pinker for *The Blank Slate*, Nathan Rosenberg and L. E. Birdzell, Jr for *How the West Grew Rich*, Rodney Stark for *For the Glory of God*, Richard Tarnas for *The Passion of the Western Mind*, Charles Taylor for *Sources of the Self*, and Peter Watson for *A Terrible Beauty* and *Ideas*. Of course, we do not agree with all the conclusions of these thinkers – and we are sure that they will not agree with us on many points – but their work has been invaluable to us. We recommend these excellent books to any reader wanting more depth on the subjects covered.

Finally, this book would never have been written without the intervention of Matthew Parris, who introduced the authors to each other. We have greatly enjoyed our collaboration and are most thankful!

A change to a new type of music is something to beware of as a hazard to all our fortunes. For the modes of music are never disturbed without unsettling of the most fundamental political and social conventions.

(Plato, *The Republic*, Book IV)

Introduction

In 1900, most citizens of the West felt tremendous pride and confidence in their civilization. There was a strong sense, common to Americans and British, to Europeans and Canadians, to Australians and New Zealanders, of belonging to a vigorous, expanding, progressive and exciting civilization, the best ever.

Today, that sense has gone. Why? Not because of economics, external events or external enemies. Despite the horrors of the first half of the last century, by most objective standards Western civilization has, since 1900, made great material, military, medical, scientific and even political progress. Westerners stopped killing and torturing each other. Western civilization saw off its two most deadly and horrific enemies, the Nazis and the communists, both of whom had been incubated in the West. If there is a crisis of the West – and we say there *is* – it is *internally* generated. It lies in the West's collapse in self-confidence. It lies in Western heads. It lies in *ideas*.

The link between ideas and events has been skilfully made by Osama bin Laden. 'The values of this Western civilization', he gloated after 9/11, 'have been destroyed. Those awesome symbolic towers that speak of liberty, human rights and humanity have been destroyed. They have gone up in smoke.' In other words, terrorism is extinguishing Western civilization, because it is crushing belief in Western values.

This is largely propaganda, or wishful thinking.

The truth is worse. Regardless of al-Qa'ida, or any other enemy of the West, its civilization is desperately threatened, because most Westerners no longer believe in the ideas that have made the West so successful. The collapse of Western self-confidence has little to do with enemies, and everything to do with seismic shifts in Western ideas and attitudes. There is therefore mercifully little in these pages about Mr bin Laden and his ilk.

Our enquiry is very simple. We ask four questions: Is there anything special about Western civilization? Why has it been so successful? Why is it now threatened? Will it survive? We answer these questions. It would spoil the plot if we gave bald answers right at the start. But we can give some hints.

Western civilization has thrived more than any other civilization of the past or present – it has been much more successful in economic, military and political terms, in science and technology, in the arts, and in enhancing its citizens' health, wealth, longevity, and even, probably, their happiness. For all its many manifest and serious faults, the West attaches more importance than other civilizations have done or do to the sanctity and dignity of human life, the education of all its people, to equality of opportunity, to the freedom of the individual and the use of his or her talents, to the essential equality and brotherhood of humankind, to the elimination of prejudice against individuals and groups, to the promotion of science and the arts, to the invention of better, cheaper and more convenient products, and to the relief of suffering. Judging by these Western standards of civilization – which Westerners may be proud to proclaim, and many of which are universal human aspirations – no other civilization has come close to Western achievements.

The West has achieved its success very largely because of a number of fundamental ideas and the actions they inspired – to deeply ingrained and often subconscious patterns of thought and behaviour. A large degree of the West's success can be traced to six principal 'ideas' or 'success factors' – Christianity, optimism, science, economic growth, liberalism and individualism. Of course, other selections of what makes the West different and dominant could be made. But careful examination of the six ideas reveals well enough the character and peculiarities of Western civilization, and provides a powerful lens for examining the West's history, power and essential unity.

A focus on the six ideas does even more. It also enables us to see, despite all the successes, what is behind the widespread lack of confidence in the West. The six success factors, which underpinned Western boldness, have suffered a century of sustained attack. By and large, these beliefs no longer inspire or unite the West, or give individuals the trust essential for unconscious co-ordinated action. We cannot, of course, help but notice the barbarians at our gates. But great civilizations rarely crumble just because of external enemies. The barbarians were only able to challenge the Roman Empire successfully once it had become decadent and divided. Hitler was only able to destroy Germany's humane and democratic civilization because the latter had too few defenders. Today also, for the West, internal divisions and flaws are the real threat. There is little appreciation of what makes the West different and uniquely valuable. Cynicism, pessimism and carelessness abound. A drift toward collective suicide is evident; it is deeply impregnated in our history since 1914. It can be traced to the declining attachment to the ideas that used to inspire the West and the world.

Our review of the six factors, however, shows that they have great resilience, and in some cases, through subtle evolution, enormous staying power. Surface impressions are often wrong. But as we examine the challenges to the six success factors in the last hundred years or so, we'll see, for each of the six, the seriousness of the threat to the West's future. For shorthand, we'll use a system of 'traffic lights' colours, using 'green' to mean 'no basic problem', yellow to mean 'danger', and red to mean 'grave and possibly terminal problem'.

One thing we can promise. This is not a dirge for a lost civilization, nor a call for a return to eternal values. If ideas are under attack, there are usually very good reasons, although not always the obvious ones. To be vibrant, ideas must evolve or be discarded as we discover more about the universe, our society and our nature. There are lots of twists and turns in our report. And the findings are by no means all gloomy.

What do we mean by 'the West'?

We mean the countries settled by Europeans, with the population comprising a clear majority of people of European descent, and with cultures and ideas largely derived from Europe. What does this mean today? Briefly, North America, Europe and Australasia.

Let us admit at the outset that 'the West' is an arbitrary and often anachronistic concept, that it is descriptively misleading, and that we are uncomfortable with many of the geographical and ideological connotations it has acquired in the last hundred years. The game of contrasting the virtuous West with the less virtuous East started with the ancient Greeks, who used 'the West' to mean Free Greece, and 'the East' to mean Persian tyranny. This is not our game, since our view of Europe (and therefore the West) includes Eastern Europe. Not only do Western and Eastern Europe share a common history, they have also both contributed important waves of emigrants to America – think, for example, of the importance of Greek, Jewish, Polish and Ukrainian communities to America.

Despite our reservations about the name, we use 'the West' and 'Western civilization' because for well over a hundred years that has been the generally accepted term for the culture and political reality of America and Europe. No serious historian or sociologist can dispute the European origins of most Americans or the similarity in culture and outlook of Europeans and Americans. Let us repeat, however, that for us 'the West' includes Eastern Europe, regions of Western Europe such as Ireland, Spain and Portugal often overlooked by 'Western' commentators, and countries such as Canada, Australia and New Zealand that mainly comprise descendants of European settlers and where European culture still predominates.

What do we mean by 'suicide'?

Individual suicide is the self-imposed end to one's life. The suicide of a civilization is the self-imposed end of that civilization. *Chambers Dictionary* gives one definition of suicide as 'the bringing about of one's own downfall, often unintentionally'.[1] That is what we mean by the possible suicide of the West – the accidental end of a great civilization wrought not by external enemies but by what Westerners do and fail to do.

We mean a failure to solve the contradictions in Western society in such a way as to preserve Western ideals. In practical terms, we mean either ecological suicide ('ecocide'), or, more likely, the transformation of Western society into another civilization, one not based on the six principal ideas we have identified as core to Western values. Germinating for the last century, but clearly evident only in the past 20 or 30 years, there are trends in Western society that, if they continue, will render it quite different – different from its historic aims and ideals, and different from the reality that had been approaching closer and closer for several hundred years. We will see the changes evident in discussing each of the six big ideas that have made Western civilization work so well, but briefly it is this – the denial of personal responsibility to improve oneself and society, the denial of all that goes with liberal ideals.

Western civilization, we will show, is dramatically different from other past or present civilizations, and it is different and more successful because of deeply rooted ideas – so deeply rooted that we don't stop to think about them – and the behaviour they elicit. At the heart of Western civilization is the restless, self-advancing, self-improving, optimistic, rational, controlling, and – yes, this too – in some sense idealistic individual, a person who is going somewhere, who believes in himself or herself and in their role in society.

---

1   One might ask how suicide can ever be unintentional, but consider common observations along the lines of 'That speech was political suicide'.

Our thesis is that the self-improving, confident and responsible individual, fully rooted in a liberal community and with a sense of duty to that community, is dying out. In place of belief we have agnosticism or relativism. In place of optimism we have fatalism. In place of a sense of progress we have premonitions. In place of dreams we have nightmares.

In place of saving and deferred gratification we have consumption. In place of striving, sentimentality. In place of responsibility to others we have, for many, the sense of being a victim; and for many more, the overwhelming drive to look after number one. In place of idealism we have cynicism. In place of meaning and purpose we have money. In place of reason we have emotions. In place of wisdom we have experts. In place of culture we have sub-cultures. In place of seriousness we have triviality and self-indulgence. In place of hard experience we have shallowness. In place of desperation, depression. In place of authentic role models we have vapid celebrities. In place of authority or consensus we have divergence. In place of community we have fragmentation.

It is not that Westerners today are worse than earlier generations. One can even argue that ethical behaviour, far from declining, has actually advanced. If we think things are bad, it is partly because we are more sensitized towards injustice, and because the standards against which we judge ourselves, and our civilization, have demonstrably progressed. Throughout the West there is now less discrimination against minority groups and against women, more help for the poor, less cruelty to children and animals, more concern for the environment, less overt racism, less harmful nationalism, and more widespread charitable giving than ever before. As a percentage of population, we kill far fewer of our own citizens and our enemies than we used to.

Our contention is not that moral standards have gone up or down – for surely they have done both – but that our ideas have *changed*, and that our *confidence in certain key ideas* has declined or in some cases almost collapsed. If the ideas we no longer believe in were responsible for our unique success as a civilization, then we are in deep trouble. We think we demonstrate that such is the case.

The heart of our investigation is whether the trends driving Western civilization toward extinction can be resisted and reversed, or whether they are structurally inevitable. Sometimes, perhaps usually, there are no good reasons for suicide, and yet it is inevitable: it is purely self-imposed, or, more precisely, imposed by the self's thoughts, at odds with a more 'sensible' view of reality. The only way to avoid suicide is to reconstruct the way we think of ourselves; and this may be impossible.

The ghosts of Spengler and Burnham

One of the most influential books of the last century was *The Decline of the West* by Oswald Spengler, a German schoolmaster.[2] The first volume was published in 1918, to huge acclaim from his fellow countrymen. Spengler's work is opaque and long-winded, but there are flashes of brilliant insight and it is stunning in its sweep and scholarship. Spengler never explained what he meant by either 'the West' or 'decline', which makes summary of his thesis impossible. No matter. What Spengler gave the world was an evocative phrase – in some sense he permanently altered the perception and self-perception of the West, associating it with decline. Western civilization, whatever was meant by that, was a temporary phenomenon, destined to fall just as it had risen.

'Decline', whatever it is, is not the same as suicide. We are not neo-Spenglerians. Since Spengler wrote, America and Europe have made enormous strides forward on almost every criterion defining the vitality of a civilization – certainly in science, in business innovation and living standards, in the humanities and arts, in all forms of music, in military power and in peace within the West. Anyone

2 Oswald Spengler (1991) *The Decline of the West*, Oxford University Press, Oxford.

arguing that the West is in decline would have to be a mental contortionist of formidable skill and sleight of hand.

In 1964, political theorist James Burnham published *Suicide of the West*, subtitled *The Meaning and Destiny of Liberalism*.[3] It's a rattling good read, and the thesis can be easily summarized. Burnham starts by observing that between 1900 and 1960 the West contracted dramatically in territory and number of people. He asks why:

> The contraction of the West cannot be explained by any lack of economic resources or of military and political power . . .
>
> We must therefore conclude that the primary causes of the contraction of the West – not the sole causes, but the sufficient and determining causes – have been internal and non-quantitative, involving either structural change or intellectual, moral and spiritual factors . . . in a way 'the will to survive'.

Burnham, once a romantic follower of Trotsky but by 1964 a romantic conservative pessimist and fierce anti-communist, explains the voluntary withdrawal of the West from empire and from confronting communism as the result of 'liberalism'. He says that the spread of liberal ideas, where 'the preferred enemy is to the Right', makes it impossible to see the challenges of the real world properly:

> The crucial present challenges are, I believe, three: first, the jungle now spreading within our own society, in particular in our great cities; second, explosive population growth and political activization within the world's backward areas, principally . . . occupied by non-white masses; third, the drive of the communist enterprise for a monopoly of world power.

---

3   James Burnham (1964, 1965) *Suicide of the West: The Meaning and Destiny of Liberalism*, Jonathan Cape, London.

Looking through the glass of liberalism it is impossible to see these challenges clearly . . .

We finish our circle at the point of beginning: Liberalism is the ideology of Western suicide . . . the ideology of modern liberalism must be understood as itself one of the expressions of Western contradiction and decline; a kind of epiphenomenon or haze accompanying the march of history; a swan song, a spiritual solace of the same order as the murmuring of a mother to a child who is gravely ill. There is really dazzling ingenuity in the liberal expression of defeat as victory, abandonment as loyalty, timidity as courage . . .

Liberalism permits Western civilization to be reconciled to its dissolution.

It should be clear from Burnham's splendid prose that, in reincarnating his title, we are not subscribing to his thesis. In our view, Burnham's premise – that the voluntary abandonment of empire presages the suicide of a civilization – is deeply flawed. In terms of a civilization built up over at least two millennia, the empire being jettisoned was of very recent origin, and entirely surplus to requirements. The nations colonized and then de-colonized, by and large, never absorbed the culture of the Western empires concerned; they were conquered and then released. Between 1875 and 1895 – a tiny interlude in Europe's long history – European imperialists planted their flags on more than a quarter of the planet's land. It is this mad aberration that needs explanation, not its reversal. Whatever the effect of de-colonization on the Third World, the West's economy subsequently went from strength to strength.

With the benefit of hindsight, we can see that Burnham had it almost exactly wrong. It was not the West that collapsed because of Western liberalism; it was communism.

Without the attraction of Western prosperity and freedom, the people of Eastern Europe would not have removed and swarmed through the Berlin Wall in 1989, nor would their Soviet masters have stood idly by and allowed their civilization to disappear of its own volition.[4]

Trends versus wishes

We have tried to divorce our own wishes from analysis of what is happening. This is not a polemic. Nor is it a history, or even a history of ideas, but rather an analysis of history and ideas to answer the four specific questions – about the success and survival of Western civilization – we posed at the start. Inevitably, our description will from time to time be coloured by our preconceptions, opinions, personal histories and experience. But only in the final chapter do we allow ourselves the luxury of giving our explicit views on the implications of our analysis. We have come to this task from very different backgrounds – a libertarian conservative businessman and a libertarian politician from the democratic left – but we reach a common conclusion, one we think is both original and important.

---

4   It is said that when Mikhail Gorbachev visited a Canadian supermarket he was
    so staggered by the goods on display that he concluded it had been specially
    constructed for his visit. When he was eventually convinced that such cornu-
    copia was commonplace, his faith in communism began to wilt.

1 The Identity of the West

The most fascinating, weighty and difficult issue facing every Westerner today is not one of economic survival but of *identity*. 'Who am I?' The paradox is that we ask the question as individuals, yet we can only define our existence and its meaning beyond our role as individuals, by reference to a *group* or *groups*. This is of course the great insight from the German philosopher Immanuel Kant (1724–1804) – that our individual essence is experienced primarily in relationships with other individuals and the world around us, while at the same time retaining its essential and unique identity. There is no obvious or correct answer to 'Who am I?', yet how Westerners generally decide to answer the question will profoundly affect the future of the West.

We are social animals. We need a sense of identity. The more decentralized society becomes, and the more individualistic each one of us becomes, the more the sense of identity matters. It is our individual decision. It is not prescribed by society. The intensification of individualism does not remove or mitigate the need for collective identity; it makes it simultaneously more elusive, more psychologically imperative, and more vital for society. Not only that – the outcome is open, and highly unpredictable.

To see the power of identity, consider what happened in Europe in the last century. In 1900, the single most salient sense of identity for most Europeans was not class, or race, or occupation, or religion, or political creed. All these sources of identity were important to many, and to European society as a whole. But the single most potent source of identity was *national*. Without that overwhelming sense of national identity, encouraged and buttressed throughout the nineteenth century by conservatives and liberals alike throughout Europe, the terrible war of 1914–18 would not have broken out, and, even if it had, would not have been allowed to continue beyond the first few months.

It was commonly believed at the outset that the war 'would be over by Christmas', within four months of starting. By Christmas 1914, however, it was clear to statesmen on all sides that the war was a surprising catastrophe for all combatants – militarily, economically, above all in terms of human lives and suffering. Yet pride in national identity was too deeply rooted throughout Europe to stop the war, until one side had eventually bludgeoned the other into exhausted submission. Eight and a half million Europeans were killed. Europe's colonial empires fell apart, its pre-eminent position in the world irretrievably lost. The Russian Revolution of 1917, a direct result of the war, had by 1953 led to around 54 million deaths from civil war, terror, gulags and political executions. Without the war of 1914–18, we almost certainly wouldn't have had the barbarities of Nazi Germany, or of the Second World War, which between them led to around 47 million further murders and deaths,[1] nearly wiping out Western civilization.

After 1945, nationalism continued to cause immense harm to the world, but mainly outside Western Europe. With American sponsorship, the creation of a 'common market' and later the European Union eradicated virulent nationalism, forging a sense of shared interest and identity between European nations. They stopped invading each other, and subscribed to a Western military alliance. Sixty years of unbroken peace and prosperity in Western Europe followed.

Yet now the kaleidoscope of Western identity is shifting in countless different conflicting and complementary ways. Identity has become personalized. It has become localized, as in Basque or

---

1 Median estimates are 14.4 million military and 27.1 million civilian deaths in the Second World War and 5.6 million in the genocide of Jews by Nazis. Based on Norman Davies (1996) *Europe: A History*, Oxford University Press, Oxford, pp. 1328–9.

Catalonian 'nationalism'. It has become sexualized, in feminist and gay and lesbian liberation movements. It has become *sportif*, in the fierce allegiance of fans – by no means always local fans – to particular football, baseball or basketball teams. It has become environmental, as Greenpeace, Friends of the Earth and other groups engage in peaceful or less peaceful action throughout the world. It has become animal-liberationist. It has become terrorist. It has become religious, in adherence to local or international churches and cults. It has become virtual, in the proliferation of online 'communities'. It has become ethnic, as in 'African-American', and sometimes language-based, as when Hispanic identity trumps nationality – Miami is said to be 'the capital of Latin America'. It has become philanthropic, in giving to or working for countless different causes. It has become political across local and national boundaries, as in anti-globalization and other single-issue movements. It has become organizational, as in identifying with one's employer and moving round the world for Shell or IBM. It has become transnational, as more and more people travel, work and have friends in foreign countries, or buy property there. It has become cosmopolitan. It has become fashion-related, age-related, school-related and celebrity-related. And, for many, identity continues to reside in traditional sources, including the family, clubs and associations, occupation, loyalty to a political party, class, race and nation.

Identity, in sum, has become multiple, fragmented, centrifugal, transient, idiosyncratic. Our identity is patched together by ourselves as individuals. But over the next few decades, Westerners will probably plump collectively for one of the following predominant forms of identity:

- A retreat into many forms of purely local and personal forms of identity, without any prevalent broader sense of community.
- A sense of local and personal identity, coupled with a revival of national identity as Americans, Germans, Australians and so forth.

- As above, except that 'Europeans' identify themselves principally as such, more than as their constituent nationalities, so that Western identity is mainly bifurcated into 'American' and 'European' loyalties.
- A sense of local and personal identity, combined with a view that we are all 'cosmopolitans', citizens of the world.
- A sense of local, personal and national identity, together with a common perception that we are citizens of the West with important common identity and interests.

Is Western identity to become a meaningless, personalized jumble? Is nationalism in the West set to rear its ugly head again? Are America and Europe to define and cherish their differences? Are we to seek the common denominator of 'world' identity, and can such a notion have any real meaning? Or does Western identity really have resonance for the future?

Any outcome except the last, we think, will make it unlikely that Westerners continue to enjoy peace, prosperity and a broadly civilized society. The currents of contemporary identity are swirling and choppy, and could easily put the West's charmed life under water. We can see both the danger and the opportunity by sketching how the 'ideas' of Europe, America and the West came about, and how viable they remain in the age of pick-and-mix identity.

The idea of Europe

Does Europe exist? Right up to the 1950s, Europe could be dismissed as just a vague and fluid geographical expression. To the extent that Europe has existed as a compelling force in history, however, it existed as an *idea*, one of the most imaginative and fruitful ideas of all time.[2]

---

2   See Peter Watson (2005) *Ideas: A History of Ideas from Fire to Freud*, Weidenfeld & Nicolson, London, pp. 319–38.

The idea of Europe emerged from an earlier great idea – that of Christendom. When the Roman Empire fell apart, all that united those formerly under its control was the idea of Christendom – that all its lands and peoples, whatever the ebbs and flows of political power, were mentally united, enjoying a common civilization. The tradition of Christianity was supplemented by a rich intellectual culture, and united by the common language of Latin, sharing the same concepts, books and recognizably similar institutions – cathedrals, monasteries, nunneries, cathedral schools, universities – across countries throughout the continent. Christendom's culture extended well beyond Christianity itself, encompassing Hellenic (ancient Greek), Roman, Islamic, Persian and Chinese influences.

The upshot was a uniquely prolific and inventive intellectual domain, leading to the world's first empirical science, unparalleled feats of technology and exploration, the colonization of 'new' continents, and eventually the conquest of hunger and untimely death. Christendom provided a sense of common allegiance and identity independent of political events, and transcending all other sources of identity, be they local, tribal, ethnic, national, political, or even, ironically, religious. Christendom did not cease to exist as a powerful idea even when the Eastern Church separated from the Roman one, when armies went off on the land-grabbing exercises they called Crusades, when there were three contending popes simultaneously, or when Europe bathed itself in bloody religious wars.

In a slow and tortuous process between 1300 and 1800, the idea of Christendom gradually evolved into the idea of Europe, which nearly always included Eastern Europe. After 1300, geographers began to make frequent references to 'Europe'. In 1458, Pope Pius II promulgated a *Treatise on the State of Europe*.[3] In the late seventeenth century, 'Europe' replaced 'Christendom' or 'the Christian Commonwealth' as the prevalent term. By the eighteenth century,

---

3   Denys Hay (1957) *Europe: The Emergence of an Idea*, Edinburgh University Press, Edinburgh.

praise of Europe had become *de rigueur* in the politically correct circles of the Enlightenment. The idea of Europe became associated with many progressive causes, among them religious toleration – a huge advance for a civilization that had recently in good conscience burnt tens of thousands of witches – political liberalism, the abatement of cruel punishments and of aggressive nationalism, universal peace, the progress of commerce and industry, and, in some quarters, the political unification of Europe, and attacks on established religion.

William Penn (1644–1718) was the first to call for a European parliament. Voltaire, in 1751, called Europe 'a kind of great republic divided into several states . . . but all corresponding with each other . . . they all have the same religious foundation . . . [and] the same principles of public law and politics, unknown in other parts of the world.' 'There are no longer Frenchmen, Germans, and Spaniards, or even English', ventured Rousseau rather optimistically in 1771, 'but only Europeans.'[4]

The idea of Europe came to describe not a geographical reality, but a universal *vision* – that of a civilized, tolerant, peaceful community, simultaneously diverse *and* united, transcending nationality and politics, grounded in scholarship and cultural advances, friendly to the arts, sciences and commerce, and advancing human dignity, freedom and happiness.

During the past 60 years, this urbane idea of Europe has found expression in a series of economic and political arrangements. Co-operation in coal and steel evolved into the Common Market and then the European Union – an engagement by proud nation states in a collaborative European endeavour designed to maintain peace, enhance prosperity, and address some of the great global issues of trade, environment, development and international cooperation.

---

4   Within three decades of this visionary remark, the European Powers were involved in a life and death struggle to prevent Napoleon uniting Europe under France.

The idea of America

America is unique in many ways, but most importantly in this: it was settled by dissidents pursuing an idea. The settlers were seventeenth- and eighteenth-century Protestants.[5] Their idea was a homogeneous Puritan community of independent citizens – God fearing, hard working, self-improving. The settlers came armed with Anglo-Protestant (and substantially British) culture, values and know-how, sharing in large part the intellectual assumptions of the European Enlightenment described above, excepting only its religious scepticism and, to some extent, its tolerance.[6]

American identity was forged by two great political upheavals: the American Revolution and the Civil War. Up to the 1750s, settlers and their descendants identified principally with the state settlements – Massachusetts, New York, Pennsylvania, or Virginia – and beyond that with 'British North America' and the lands from which they came. It was only with the events leading up to the War and Declaration of Independence that American national identity began to emerge, heavily associated with a political creed proclaiming the equality and individuality of free Americans. Nonetheless, state loyalties remained most salient right up to the Civil War. It was only after this cataclysm, from the 1860s to the 1950s, that American national identity became paramount for most Americans. Reflecting its origins in two traumatic political conflicts, it was a very 'political' form of nationalism, pulsating

---

5   The politically active population of the US in 1790 was 100 per cent white, 98 per cent Protestant and 80 per cent British (the rest nearly all German or Dutch).

6   It would be anachronistic to claim that Enlightenment figures such as Voltaire, Diderot or Rousseau believed in a multiracial society, but all three stressed the essential equality of humankind, regardless of religion, race or nationality. Europeans had the advantage of a continent that had been free of slavery and mass migration for hundreds of years. Americans had the curse of slavery, thanks to European and African slave traders. In 1790, 15 per cent of the American population were black slaves.

with passion for 'the American way' – a set of beliefs that came to be second nature to most free Americans.

What were these beliefs? They were grounded in the radical political ideas of seventeenth- and eighteenth-century Europe, and in Puritanism. In 1944, political scientist Gunnar Mydral defined the 'American creed': 'the essential dignity of the individual human being, of the fundamental equality of all men, and of certain inalienable rights to freedom, justice, and a fair opportunity'. The reality hasn't always matched up to the ideals, of course; but the fundamental values that built America ring out, like the Liberty Bell itself, loud and clear.

The idea of the West

The idea of the West is no more, and no less, than the idea of America combined with the idea of Europe. The idea of Europe is that of a civilized, peaceful, prosperous community of diverse nations united by common geography and ideas. The idea of America is the unification of European settlers, and mainly European immigrants, and now also people of Hispanic origin, through a common commitment to political ideals – of freedom, equal status and opportunity. The idea of the West is the common cause of America and Europe in helping each other and in standing up for freedom and human dignity.

If this 'idea of the West' currently provokes a puzzled or cynical reaction from many Westerners and non-Westerners alike; this is not because the 'idea of the West' lacks historical validity or attractiveness, but because some Americans and some Europeans have betrayed or drifted away from the ideas and ideals that have made Western civilization so attractive and successful. There would have been no confusion or cynicism about the idea of the West in the years after the Second World War. Since then the West has gained hugely in economic unity, prosperity and military force, but declined markedly in social cohesion, moral force, certainty of purpose and mutual support and sympathy between America and Europe – to the point where the 'idea of the West' needs either to be redefined and reasserted, or abandoned for ever.

The discovery of America changed the course of history and hugely enriched Europeans economically, politically, socially and intellectually in the short, medium and long term. The discovery of the New World gave a huge boost to Europe, providing silver for trade with the East, a new frontier for agriculture and industry, and the growth in living standards that flowed from mass production for a massively enlarged market. America offered a fresh life for tens of millions of Europeans, including many who were oppressed, desperate or destitute. For four centuries, America furnished a safety valve for European societies; and for two centuries a new model of freedom that eventually triumphed throughout Europe. The pivotal force driving history forward in the past half millennium has been the common interests and complementary genius of Americans and Europeans.

The intellectual foundation of the ideas is identical – Christianity, optimism, science, growth, liberalism, individualism. Yet the idea of Europe and the idea of America share something even more powerful than a complex compound of interlocking ideas. Both the idea of Europe and the idea of America involve a collective emotional commitment to a broad community, to geographical and historical roots, and to an evolving ideal. The ideas and the ideals are common; the history and peoples overlap; only the geographies are different. The idea of the West encompasses all the ideas, all the ideals, all the history, and both continents, together with the other European settlements in Australasia

The idea of the West is not new, although it was only in the twentieth century that it acquired compelling political traction, often under unfortunate circumstances. From the start, 'the West' combined political and cultural connotations. The phrase was first used in modern times by Anglophile Americans to emphasize the common language, civilization and interests of the United States and the British Empire in the years before the First World War when the two economies were deeply entwined. The war was important in cementing and re-creating links between Europeans and Americans, not least because it took three million American servicemen over to Europe.

In the early twentieth century, the precise geographical definition of 'the West' was opaque, sometimes including the whole of Europe and sometimes being confined to North America, the British Empire, and (usually) France. Oswald Spengler's *Decline of the West* was always ambiguous about the countries that were slated for decline, referring in places to 'European–American Civilization' and in other places to 'West-European', which clearly excluded Germany. Yet in discussing Western civilization, Spengler consistently included Italians and Germans, liberally sprinkling his text with 'our' and 'we', implying a common Western cultural heritage shared by the German writer and his German readers.

When the Iron Curtain divided Europe from 1947, 'the West' came to exclude Soviet-run Eastern Europe. Happily, by 1991, with the tearing down of the Berlin Wall and the return of most Eastern European countries to autonomy and 'Western' styles of democracy and market economies, it was possible once more to speak of a 'West' that embraced the whole of Europe, politically as well as culturally.

Does 'the West' really exist?

The idea of the West, incorporating the idea of Europe and the idea of America, re-made the map of the world during the last century. At immense cost, the destructive nationalism that pitted Europeans against Europeans was largely extirpated. The anti-Western ideologies of Nazism and communism were also vanquished. Politically, 'the West' has come to mean a diverse set of free and independent European nations, still retaining their own parliaments and national identities but united economically and to a degree politically, at peace with each other and in broad alliance with the United States. Inevitably there are sometimes serious strains in some of these relationships. Yet, in terms of peace, prosperity and freedom, this is probably the best possible solution that could have emerged for all the European and American peoples.

Political events shape identity, but political events alone cannot sustain identity. Ultimately, 'the West' only exists as a meaningful idea if there are important and deeply held attitudes and beliefs that differentiate 'the West' from 'the Rest', and if those attitudes and beliefs are widely shared within the constituent parts of the West.

We say that there are. Westerners, be they Americans or Canadians, Poles or French, Australians or New Zealanders, British, Italians, Irish, Spanish or Finnish, or from any other Western country, think and act in ways that are broadly similar and that are different from the ways that most Japanese or Chinese, Arabs or Africans, Indians or Malaysians think and act. We will explain the difference between the West and the Rest in terms of history, culture and beliefs in the West that derive ultimately from a cluster of common, interlocking ideas, our six 'success factors'.

Other writers have adopted different categories but come to broadly similar conclusions. Oswald Spengler identified the restless dynamism of the West with a view of morality that required world improvement and personal striving:

> Western mankind, without exception, is under the influence of an immense optical illusion. Everyone *demands* something of the rest . . . In the ethics of the West everything is direction, claim to power, and the will to affect the distant. Here Luther is completely at one with Nietzsche, Popes with Darwinians, Socialists with Jesuits . . . What we have completely failed to observe is the peculiarity of moral dynamics [in the West].[7]

---

7 Spengler (1991), p. 176.

Sociologist Daniel Bell talks of 'individualism, achievement, and equality of opportunity'. Gunnar Myrdal highlights 'the essential dignity of the individual human being'. The essence of the West is an indefinable blend of rationalism, activism, confidence, knowledge-seeking, personal responsibility, self-improvement, world-improvement and compassion. At the root of it all is a sense of ethical individualism that is shared by Europeans and their descendants, and represented today by the peoples of America, Europe and Australasia.

We do not say that this ethical individualism is wholly good in its origins or its results. In fact, it is highly dangerous, and constantly needs to be tamed by common sense and a humility that is often missing. To use Spengler's wonderful adjective, Western ethical individualism is 'Faustian'. It is power-seeking and enormously disruptive – of established authority, cultures, traditions, belief systems, pre-industrial ways of life, and even of the planet's whole ecological poise. Westerners never know when to leave things alone. They are always going too far, too fast. They always want to *do something*, when often the best thing is to do nothing. In their wish to improve, they intrude, and they often leave things worse than they found them. They are insensitive, impatient, domineering. They are always opinionated, and often intolerant. They bulldoze. They want to convert, to persuade, to make changes. They do not like to acknowledge any limit to their immense powers.

Whether good or bad, however, the West's ethical individualism is common to Western people and largely absent from non-Western peoples, except where they have been influenced by the West. As the work of sociologist Geert Hofstede demonstrates unambiguously, all Western nations are highly individualistic and no non-Western society comes anywhere close on this dimension.[8]

---

8   On Hofstede's scoring method, the average for Western countries was 66.7 and the average for non-Western countries was only 25.7. Geert Hofstede, *Culture's Consequences: Comparing Values, Behaviors, Institutions, and Organizations Across Nations*, Sage Publications, Thousand Oaks, Calif., 1980, revised edition, 2001. For more detail on Hofstede's findings, see Chapter 7 below.

National, universal, or Western identity?

In Europe, toxic nationalism is largely a relic, discredited by the horrors of the two 'European civil wars' and eroded by the success, even if often only grudgingly admitted, of European institutions and identity. European nations, on the whole, are no longer disposed to invade each other and they believe that their economic interests are mainly complementary. Against the disasters of the first half of the twentieth century, and the division and oppression later symbolized by the Iron Curtain, the emergence of a Europe largely united economically, with some common political institutions but still retaining national parliaments and diverse national and sub-national identities, appears about the best possible realistic outcome.

In the United States, though for largely different reasons, nationalism and national identity have also declined. The Civil Rights movement of the 1950s and 1960s brought black Americans into full equal citizenship, but also created separate black and 'African-American' consciousness. The Vietnam War, both deeply unpopular and unsuccessful, weakened American national identity, as large numbers of young Americans avoided or evaded the draft, some even renouncing American nationality. Huge numbers of Mexican and other Hispanic immigrants have settled in the US in the past three decades and, unlike earlier immigrants, they have retained close links to their home base, often remaining Spanish speaking and having dual nationality or citizenship; many observers believe that America is evolving towards a bi-cultural, bi-lingual society. As already noted, the advance of individualism has become associated with a turning towards inward and self-defined identities, resulting in a shift from an engagement with the nation to one with smaller and more homogeneous groupings. The decline in communal identity, and in trust in political leaders, has also weakened national allegiance. Finally, as Samuel Huntington has noted, 'elements of America's intellectual, political, and business elites increasingly downgraded their commitment to their nation and gave privilege to trans-national and sub-national claims on their loyalties'.

The events of '9/11' led to a dramatic revival of American nationalism, but this appears to have been an exceptional and temporary spike in a long, downwards trend. The sapping of national confidence that has resulted from the war in Iraq and the continued insurgency there, and from the federal failure to help the (largely black and poor) people left behind in New Orleans after hurricane Katrina in 2005, have again weakened the sense that America is a united, confident nation.

Cosmopolitan or 'universal' world identity is at least a theoretical alternative to nationalism. During the 1980s and early 1990s it became fashionable to argue that 'modernism' and 'Westernism' had become so pervasive and influential that we were all living in one vast global village, although perhaps 'global shopping mall' would have been a less inapt description. On closer inspection, however, cosmopolitanism is either extremely shallow or a complete chimera.

As many scholars have documented, and geopolitical events have demonstrated, humans do not normally 'think globally'. Local, national and regional culture, history, religion and politics are not ready to be swept into a wastebasket labelled 'History'; those who imagined otherwise are experiencing nasty shocks. Sociologists and psychologists who have studied the way different nations think find, time and time again, the same pattern – a common Western template, and a handful of other less homogeneous regional patterns of thought, usually classified with varying degrees of conviction and manipulation into categories such as Chinese, Japanese, Hindu, Buddhist, Islamic, Latin American, African, and Orthodox/Russian. The thesis of a 'clash of civilizations', propounded by Samuel Huntington in 1993,[9] increasingly

---

9   In an article in *Foreign Affairs*, summer 1993, entitled 'The Clash of Civilizations?', subsequently expanded into Samuel P. Huntington (1996) *The Clash of Civilizations and the Remaking of the World Order*, The Free Press, New York.

looks ingenious but forced, exaggerating the degree of similarity within each 'civilization' and the necessity for the civilizations to clash;[10] but at least the ensuing controversy has highlighted cultural differences and the often unfortunate consequences of diverse national, regional and religious identities beyond the West.

If nationalism and cosmopolitanism are poor and/or weak solutions to the need for more than private definitions of identity, perhaps the only alternative, and certainly the most logical one, is Western identity. Although Western identity necessarily requires Americans and Europeans to downplay their own separate national or regional identities, Western identity has five compelling advantages.

First, Western identity is grounded in a common history and geography, and a set of national identities that have many similarities.

Second, it goes with the flow of historical, economic and political events in the twentieth century and today – the unification of Europe, the dominant importance of trade within the Western bloc, and the intertwining of Western political, economic and military organizations and alliances.

Third, Western identity reflects the reality that there is a common mentality shared by all Westerners and not shared by non-Westerners.

Fourth, Western identity is broad enough to allow for the celebration of ethnic, local and national differences, and of various sub-national and trans-national European and American identities, while also being robust enough to mean something. Western identity is 'ethnically ecumenical' – it does not detract from Hispanic, black, Jewish, Irish, Anglo-Saxon, or any other North American or European identity; and it certainly does not pit one

---

10 Huntington also neglects the extent to which nations and groups within 'similar' civilizations themselves clash. As historian Niall Ferguson has said of the Middle East, it demonstrates 'not so much a clash of civilizations as a civilization of clashes'. Niall Ferguson (2004) *Colossus: The Rise and Fall of the American Empire*, Penguin, London.

ethnic or national group against another, or Americans against
Europeans. It allows all these groups and many others – including
even determined multiculturalists – to feel deeply about their
diverse identities without having to deny the need for broader
community associations, or to denigrate or detract from other
sources of identity.

Finally, Western identity has substantial ethical and social
content, asserting the reality of a common community, rooted
geographically, with a rich cultural heritage centred on ideals of
human worth, responsibility and potential. Western identity
allows everyone, of whatever political, religious or lifestyle affilia-
tion, to feel part of an inclusive and catholic community that
embraces diversity and individuality, yet which is also bigger than
any individual and therefore helps to give meaning to his or her
life.

Conclusion

Identity matters. In the last century, nationalism inflicted untold
harm in Europe, leading to terrible wars and barbaric regimes. In
contrast to bloody nationalism, Western civilization rests on the
very similar 'ideas' of Europe and America as communities of free,
compassionate and responsible individuals. If those values are to go
forward, and a positive sense of peace-loving communities is to be
maintained, the citizens of the West must find a space in their
hearts and minds for allegiance to the West, to the combination
and alliance of America and Europe and other ex-European settlements.

The alternative to Western identity is either some form of
identity that divides the West, and that, on history's formbook, is
likely to lead to an unpleasant and dangerous world; or it is no
common collective identity at all. If the latter, we would reach a
state of affairs that has not existed in the West for more than two
millennia; the consequences are likely to be, in Thomas Hobbes'

bleakly arresting words, 'the war of all against all . . . and the life of man, solitary, poor, nasty, brutish, and short'.[11]

Why is Western identity so powerful and so different from the identity of other civilizations? The answer lies in the West's unique history, the shared experience of six hugely potent and distinctive Western ideas. The first idea we examine is Christianity, which was also the bedrock of the other ideas. It turns out that the nature and impact of Christianity – on the West and the world generally – have been profoundly misunderstood.

---

11 Thomas Hobbes (1651) *Leviathan*.

2   Christianity

Nothing is more fundamental to the successes, excesses and failures of the West than Christianity. Yet Christians and unbelievers may be equally surprised to discover how Christianity upended the ancient world, transformed the relations of heaven and earth, and still defines our way of life and our very personalities. The story is not the one usually told; it is far more intriguing, personal, liberating and disturbing.

Though churchmen and rulers throughout the ages have struggled to deny the reality, Christianity was – and is – a far from normal religion. It was original in three respects: it made God personal and available to individuals; it made ordinary people supremely and dangerously important; and it made self-improvement of individuals, in accordance with divine purposes, the be-all and end-all of the universe. In short, the original version of Christianity was blasphemous, revolutionary, individualistic, open-ended, egalitarian, activist and optimistic, intolerant; universal yet divisive; above all hugely engaging and challenging for anyone caught up in its whirlwind.

Christianity was the world's first *individualized, activist self-help movement*.[1] It is also the main reason why all Westerners – whether

---

1   About 400 to 700 years before Christ, many religious innovators and philosophers, including the Buddha and others in India, the Hebrew prophets and Confucius in China, advocated personal holiness or other forms of self-awareness, denounced the power of priests, and/or sought to turn religion from outward show to inner conviction. But Christianity was the first religion that made *individual salvation* and *the transformation of personal behaviour* its central tenets, the first to preach that such salvation was available to *everyone in the*

Christians, agnostics, atheists, or even devotees of other religions – see the world differently and behave differently than non-Westerners; and why the West has been more successful than the 40 or 50 other civilizations ever established on our planet. If we wish to fathom the power, glory and contradictions of the West, and its profoundly misunderstood trajectory, we cannot do better than start with Christianity.

The roots of Christianity

Though it was an explosive and quite new phenomenon, Christianity did not arise in a kind of religious Big Bang. Like most astounding innovations, Christianity compounded two pre-existing powerful ideas and streams of thought: one Jewish, the other Greek.

The Jews believed that history was moving forward, that God acted in history to achieve his purpose on earth, and that they, the Chosen People, were essential actors in God's drama. Other religions had very many gods, each with their own agenda but none very much interested in people at large. But Yahweh, the Jewish God, *was* deeply involved with human history, driving it toward a golden future, using the Jews to get there. The Hebrews believed that their history would have immense spiritual consequences for the whole world. They enjoyed a unique and direct hotline to the one all-powerful God. Awareness of this link implied an unusual moral seriousness – human actions determined the future. In the centuries before Christ, a succession of eloquent prophets called for moral regeneration, social justice and compassion for the poor and downtrodden, beginning to suggest that individuals were accountable to God for their deeds. The prophets

world, and the first to base its expansion on *indiscriminate evangelization of everyone* it could reach. As such it was an individualized, activist self-help *movement* in a way that no other religion had ever been, and in its first 300 years it grew at a rate no religion had ever done before.

anticipated the 'Messiah', a charismatic, divine leader who would appear at the end of time to lead both history and the Jews to a wonderful triumphal climax.

At roughly the same time as the great Old Testament prophets, Greek philosophers developed a parallel but different view of humanity's role in the cosmos, a view more abstract, more scientific, yet also deeply spiritual. Leading Greek thinkers held that the world was a kind of super-mind, an ordered cosmos run by and expressing a pervasive intelligence, evident in the design of nature, and accessible to the fully developed human mind and soul. The ground of truth was to be found in the present world of human experience, not in some unverifiable non-human world. Although the Greeks' world-view was very different from that of the Jews, it implied a similar activist conclusion – humans should be autonomous and take charge of their destinies. Human and divine purposes could harmonize. 'The gods did not reveal, from the beginning, all things to us,' declared Xenophanes, 'but in the course of time, through seeking, men find that which is better.' Plato taught that knowledge of the divine was buried within every human soul. Human appreciation of light, truth and goodness was imperfect and half-forgotten, but the intellect could light up knowledge of the divine, and even attain divine immortality.

The most innovative new religion

Christianity combined and magnified the Jewish and Greek ideas, producing a world-view much stranger and more startling, yet incomparably more potent than either.

God becomes intimate with humanity by sending his son Jesus, the Jewish Messiah, into time and place. Jesus, both human and divine, dies a crucified criminal at the hands of Jewish and Roman justice. But this is no defeat. Jesus overcomes death and resumes his place with God. The life, death and resurrection of Jesus are the central events in all human history. It reveals God reaching out to humanity, becoming a person, suffering without complaint, demonstrating his love for individual humans, and redeeming those who sign up to the new religion, giving them happiness both in this world and to an infinitely greater degree after death . . . saving them from the eternal damnation and suffering that awaits non-believers.

Jesus starts as a somewhat conventional Jewish teacher. God works in history, using a combination of divine and human actions to demonstrate God's purpose, bringing history to a glorious end. Less conventional, yet well within the Jewish heritage, is the stress on God's compassion, empathy, love; concern for the poor, the outsider and those on the margins of society; and his ability and wish to redeem flawed humanity. Also within the prophetic tradition, though given unprecedented force by Jesus, is the call for individuals to respond to God, clean up their act and show compassion and love in their daily lives. A novel and compelling twist is given by the *reason* and *means* to improve one's character – the perfect model provided by God in Christ, the evidence of God's love for us, the example of how to love one's enemies, and the ability to tap into Christ's power to improve behaviour.

Quite outside the Jewish tradition, though not perhaps incompatible with it, is the new idea of a *suffering God*. The values of the world are turned upside down. God deploys his greatest influence not by a show of divine power – which he did throughout Jewish history – but through the most extreme form of love, demonstrated by enduring and defeating torture.

This message had great originality, considerable consistency with Jewish beliefs, and some appeal to a Jewish audience; yet none at all to the average Greek or Roman. Whichever way you cut it, it was not Rome-friendly. Like classical Judaism, it denied all the Roman gods, claiming there was only one God, the Jewish one. Like other Jews, the first Christians refused to observe the Roman state religion, with its animal sacrifice and temple worship, civil rituals and public holidays. Far worse, the new religion worshipped a dead Jew as the Son of God; and the man chosen, whatever his personal qualities, was a loser, a criminal awarded the most cruel form of Roman justice. The urbane Roman might regard Christianity as a minor, if bizarre, Jewish cult; but to the ordinary man in the forum, if he noticed it at all, it was insulting and offensive.

So nearly all the first Christians were Jews. They observed Jewish worship, rituals and food laws. In the decade after his death, Jesus' cult looked set to stagnate, one of many small and obscure Jewish sects.

But wait. Christianity was about to receive its Greek influences and become the most powerful idea on earth. Who was responsible for turbo-charging, and in very large part *creating*, Christianity? Three remarkable men active in the second half of the first century – Paul of Tarsus, a Greek-educated Jew; Luke, who was not a Jew at all; and 'John', the author of the fourth Gospel.[2]

Paul was active in the forties, fifties and early sixties CE. He was the first Christian to write anything about the new religion, which he changed and shaped. Paul never met Jesus. Paul showed remarkably little interest in Jesus' life; in all his letters, there are only half a dozen references to what Jesus did or said. It was the *idea* of *Christ*, the *risen Christ*, that commanded Paul's attention. For Paul, Jesus was not an ordinary man, but the *eternal* Son of God. The nature of God only became fully apparent in Christ, who reconciled the human world with the divine.

Luke's Gospel and his Acts of the Apostles – which were longer than all Paul's writings, and comprised almost a quarter of what became the New Testament – were written for Greeks and Romans. They told how Christianity moved beyond its Jewish heritage and became a *universal* religion.

Luke's story was as much about Paul as Jesus. Paul wanted to preach to those outside the Jewish faith and allow them to become Christians, excusing them from Jewish food taboos and other

2   See Keith Hopkins (1999) *A World Full of Gods: Pagans, Jews and Christians in the Roman Empire*, Orion, London; and Andrew Welburn (1991) *The Beginnings of Christianity: Essene Mystery, Gnostic Revelation and the Christian Vision*, Floris Books, Edinburgh.

cultic requirements. Peter, appointed by Jesus to carry on his work, was strongly against this. Then, in Luke's account, Peter had a dream. He saw a sheet let down from heaven, full of 'animals and reptiles and birds' that Jews held to be 'unclean'. A voice from heaven commanded Peter to eat them. He protested. He was told again to eat: 'do not call anything impure that God has made clean'. Peter got the message: Christianity is to go multicultural and multiracial. Peter welcomed a prominent non-Jew, Cornelius, as a fully-fledged Christian. 'I now realize,' Peter said, 'how true it is that God does not show favouritism, but accepts men and women from every nation.'[3]

In preaching to Greeks and Romans, Paul reinterpreted the message. He made it compatible with the Greek view that the world was an ordered cosmos, about which humankind was learning more and more. Christ, said Paul, opened the way to God. Through Christ, men and women could *understand the nature of the universe and of God*, and even *gain access to God.*

Paul's idea was fully developed by another writer, 'John', author of the fourth and incomparably great and profound Gospel. The identity of John is a mystery.[4] It is thought that, like Luke, he wrote in Ephesus (now in Turkey), although later than Luke, probably around the turn of the century. John began his account in gripping style: 'In the beginning was the *Logos*.' Every educated Roman, and anyone else steeped in Greek culture, knew the idea of the *Logos* and could now instantly connect to the story. The tale of a crucified Jew was repositioned as a masterpiece of topical Greek philosophy.

Philo of Alexandria, an older contemporary of Jesus and Paul, had already devised a Jewish–Greek synthesis based around the *Logos* concept. *Logos*, Philo said, meant God's Ideas. *Logos* could be

---

3   Acts of the Apostles, 10.34–35.
4   Many scholars believe that the fourth Gospel was inspired and authorized by John Zebedee, the former fisherman who became 'the beloved disciple', but written by a Greek-trained theologian, possibly John the Elder, a follower of John Zebedee.

understood in three ways: the central Idea driving the universe; the Agent of Creation; and the Agent through which Man could *understand* God. In one brilliant stroke, John made *Christ* the *Logos*, humanizing and personalizing God and enabling him to be understood in Philo's three ways. Christ was the intelligence ordering the cosmos; *and* its Creator; *and* the way humans could comprehend and reach God. John's conceptual breakthrough was totally consistent with Paul's earlier preaching, but took it to a sublime new level. John reinterpreted and deified Jesus in a way that nobody had previously dared. The details of the historical Jesus became the mere backdrop for a majestic, liberating view of Man and God, totally unconstrained by history, geography, race, creed or culture. Men and women could share in the nature of God, because every human possessed within them the divine spark.

This was when everything began to explode. All the strange Jewish ideas behind Christianity were translated into a Greek conceptual framework, making the new religion more intellectually sophisticated, yet also more personally appealing, accessible to ordinary people, the uneducated and illiterate. New Christianity comprised *one overarching belief*, and *four practical action implications*, each of which has reverberated volcanically through history:

- The *overarching belief* was that God became man, lived, suffered, died and rejoined the divine realm. This wonderful news moved humankind and God together.
- The *first action implication* was a massive elevation of *individual personal development and responsibility*.
- The *second action implication* was the *power* behind self-improvement – the startling claim that all believers could tap directly into God's love, and even become part of God.
- The *third action implication* was an unprecedented *commitment to the poor, the dispossessed and the outsiders*.
- The *final action implication* of Christianity is less happy. The early Christians had a burning sense that conversion to

Christianity made the difference between eternal happiness and eternal torture. Hence it became the first and most successful missionary religion.

The overarching belief – God became Man

As a result, the whole course of human history, and the potential fate of everyone on earth, shifted immeasurably for the better. 'The *Logos* became flesh and dwelt among us', revealing God's infinite love for humankind. Because of this single event, the eternal became historical, the divine became personal, and individual lives – even those of quite unexceptional, ordinary folk – became supremely important. All men and women could access the divine nature; the Spirit of God could dwell within them.

Action implication 1: take personal responsibility

The Hebrews, like every other tribe, originally believed that guilt or innocence belonged to whole tribes, not to individuals.[5] But during the Hebrews' exile in Babylon, in the sixth century before Christ, the prophet Ezekiel declared that responsibility rested with the *individual*, not the family or tribe.[6] Later prophets elaborated the theme – personal responsibility was sanctioned by God. Individual responsibility went beyond observing the law; it also required acts of compassion and social justice.

The Christians extended both Jewish and Greek views of humankind's potential, but went much, much further. Jesus, Paul, John and other evangelists insisted that every individual they confronted – women as well as men – should assume the responsibilities of inner freedom. The Jewish birthright of access to God's purpose and love was made personal and universal. Through Christ, God suddenly acquired a new location – inside people, in

---

5 In Exodus 20.4–6, the sins of the fathers 'shall be visited upon the children to the third and fourth generation'. Whole families are destroyed when the patriarch dies (for example, Joshua 7).

6 'The soul who sins is the one who will die. The son will not share the guilt of the father, nor will the father share the guilt of the son' (Ezekiel 18.20).

the human self, the human soul. Paul was the first to state clearly that Christ can live inside each believer. Talking to the Athenians, Paul reframed Christianity in Greek-friendly terms:

> Paul, standing in the middle of the market, said:
> . . . God is not far from each of us,
> For 'in him we live and move and have our being',
> As even some of your poets have said,
> 'for we are indeed his offspring'.[7]

Paul wrote to Christians in Corinth: 'Your body is a temple of the Holy Spirit within you.'[8] Another early Christian went even further: 'God is Love, and he who lives in Love, lives in God, and God lives in him.'[9] According to St Peter, individual believers could 'become partakers of the divine nature'.[10]

The idea of individuality was emphasized in a new way, linked both to God, and to a moral imperative to improve oneself. Individuality meant development – an obligation, fostered by awareness of God's amazing, unlimited love, to become a better and more useful person.

It is difficult for us today to grasp quite what a breakthrough, what an astonishing and counter-intuitive world-view, this notion of personal and individual potential and obligations was at the time. It started with the totally original Christian claim that the all-powerful God, maker of heaven and earth, *was deeply interested in the well-being of every individual person in the world*. 'God so loved the world, that he sent his only Son' to earth, to suffer and save not humankind at a collective level, but individual humans. Salvation operated at the level of the single person. For the first time ever, Christians believed in a *personal* God, able to relate to separate humans. The Christian God had a direct and deep interest in

---

7 Acts of the Apostles 17.22, 27–9.
8 1 Corinthians 6.19–20.
9 1 John 4.16.
10 2 Peter 1.4.

human matters, and an urgent interest in every human being, whatever their status or nationality.

To Greeks or Romans, the concept that God – any god – cared about individuals, still less about what they did, was simply unbelievable. Even many early Christians, especially if they were not Jewish, found this belief difficult to swallow.[11] Yet the mainstream Christian view of personal responsibility before God prevailed, transforming the course of Western history.

Action implication 2: use Christ's power to change

Christianity *required* a new way of life, based around love, usefulness ('service') to other people, and the full development of the individual's powers. Never before had religion demanded such individual commitment. But Christianity also *provided the means, the technology*, for the new way of life. This too was profoundly individualized. It was not a matter of rules and regulations, or conformity to religious authority. God implanted in each Christian a sense of right and wrong, a conscience, an awareness of the self and knowledge of what to strive for. Even better, Christ gave the individual Christian a direct route to and from God.

Paul was excited by the idea of the freedom that Christ gave to the individual. He wrote to the Christians in Galatia, 'even so we, when we were children, were in bondage under the elements of the world . . . now, in Christ, we are free'.[12] Through access to divine power in Christ, the personality could draw on its own inner resources, put there by God, thus achieving confidence and freedom of action as an autonomous individual.

Nobody, Paul insisted, was outside the acceptance and love of Christ – not the sinner, the outcast, or even Jesus' murderers. Paul suffered from a deep sense of his own guilt and depravity. He experienced the grace of God through Christ, and invented the idea of

---

11 For example, Marcion, the radical Christian innovator and Gnostic (believer in esoteric knowledge) who was highly influential in the mid-second century, said that God did not care how individuals lived.

12 Galatians 4.3.

surrender to God's unconditional love as the way to remove guilt and start living properly: 'for the love of God controls us'.[13] It was futile to try to improve by one's own efforts; only surrender to a greater force – one wholly comprised of love – would work.

Luke conveyed the same message in a different form. He told how the Holy Spirit entered the disciples on the Day of Pentecost. The human and the divine could merge. Christ's followers could achieve miracles even greater than those of Jesus, through the force of the Christ Spirit. Under Greek influence, this eventually became the idea of the 'soul', the idea that everybody possessed within them a personalized and eternal essential self, which connected them to the divine realm and enabled them to improve themselves.[14]

By the fourth century, the theologian Athanasius dared to take the idea of divine inspiration to its logical conclusion. 'God', he said, 'became man in order that we become God.' Christians later saw the unfolding of God's power in all that humankind achieved in science, medicine and liberal civilization.

Action implication 3: help the underdog

Jesus focused to a remarkable extent on sinners, prostitutes, the oppressed, the sick and lame, foreigners and Gentiles. All were loved by God; all were worthy of respect.

---

13 2 Corinthians 5.14.

14 The early Christians did not talk about the 'soul' – the word can scarcely be found in the entire New Testament – and they believed in *bodily* resurrection after death. They did, however, talk about the inner life, and about 'God', 'Christ' and the 'Holy Spirit' living within and directing Christians. The idea of the soul, which had a long although often vague pre-history, became influential in Christianity through its Greek influences, and especially through that of Plato and Pythagoras, who had propagated the idea of the *immortal* soul. It should be noted, though, that most Greeks did not believe in rewards and punishments after death. Christianity was the first religion to state consistently that eternal salvation and damnation were the only alternatives. The idea of the Christian 'soul' later became a convenient repository of individualized spirituality and a bridge to the modern concept of the 'self'. Both the 'soul' and the 'self' were quite accurate, if anachronistic, reflections of the original Christian view that God could live within every human being and change his or her behaviour in a totally personalized and individual way.

Paul gave the first statement of humankind's equality and fraternity ever recorded. 'There is', he said, 'neither Jew nor Greek, slave nor free, male nor female, for you are all one in Christ Jesus.'[15]

The next account of Jesus came from Mark. His short Gospel was full of stories of Jesus healing outcasts – a paralytic man, a demon-possessed vagrant skulking in the cemetery, a suffering woman, a dying child, a deaf and mute man, two blind men, a boy with an evil spirit. Jesus fed two huge crowds. He chose humble folk as his disciples. He praised a poor widow. He refused to ignore a group of insignificant children, 'for the kingdom of God belongs to such as these.' The only person he couldn't help was a rich young man, whom Jesus loved, advising him to 'go, sell everything you have and give to the poor . . . then come, follow me. At this the man's face fell. He went away sad, because he had great wealth.'[16]

For all his Jewish perspective, Matthew began his Gospel by bringing non-Jewish stargazers to baby Jesus, and closed it with the risen Christ telling the apostles to 'go and make disciples of all nations'.[17]

Luke's Gospel added the good Samaritan, the prodigal son, the rich fool, the lost sheep, the unjust judge, and the proud Pharisee who was unfavourably contrasted to the humble tax-collector. At Nazareth, Jesus quoted from Isaiah: God 'has anointed me to preach good news to the poor . . . to proclaim freedom for prisoners, and recovery of sight for the blind, to release the oppressed . . .'[18]

It's true that all the world's great religions stress social justice and concern for the poor. But of all faiths, primitive Christianity was the most radical, egalitarian and inclusive, smashing down all barriers between people, and even the barrier between individuals and God. It is no accident that the West was the only civilization ever to abolish the slave trade and slavery voluntarily; the first to

---

15 Galatians 3.28.
16 Mark 10.21–2.
17 Matthew 28.19.
18 Luke 4.18.

abolish hunger and largely conquer untimely death; the first to put
in place frameworks of social support for citizens; and the first to
award freedom and equality to ordinary men, and later to women,
and to begin removing discrimination against minorities defined
by race, colour, disability or sexual preference.

Action implication 4: save the damned

From the very start, Christianity was both universal – anyone
could be saved – and divisive – the saved versus the damned. There
is a passionate intolerance, bordering on violence, implicit in the
Christian genes right from the start, dramatically in tension with
Christianity's other emphasis on love and self-sacrifice.

Matthew exemplified this dark heritage. He portrayed Jesus
driving traders away from the Temple, 'overturning the tables of
the money-changers and the benches of those selling doves'.[19] He
reported Jesus saying, 'Do not suppose that I have come to bring
peace to the earth. I did not come to bring peace, but a sword. For
I have come to turn "a man against his father, and a daughter
against her mother, a daughter-in-law against her mother-in-law –
a man's enemies will be the members of his own household".'[20]

It is Matthew's account that had Jesus denouncing cities that
didn't listen to him: 'Woe to you, Korazin! Woe to you, Bethsaida!
. . . It will be more bearable for Tyre and Sidon on the day of
judgment than for you . . .'[21]

Matthew was keen on hell, gnashing of teeth and eternal punishment in burning pits. The later doctrine of 'the elect' – the idea
that only a few will be saved, while most of humanity is consigned
to the flames of hell – can be traced to the parable in Matthew of
the narrow and wide gates.[22]

John's Gospel, written when orthodox Jews were excommuni-
cating Jewish Christians, had a terrible anti-Semitic streak. John

---

19 Matthew 21.12.
20 Matthew 10.34–6. Jesus is quoting Micah 7.6.
21 Matthew 11.20–4.
22 Matthew 7.13.

had Jesus telling the Jews, 'You are from below . . . you belong to your father, the devil, and you want to carry out your father's desire. He was a murderer from the beginning.'[23]

The tendency to impose right ideas by force, to divide the world into the sheep and the goats, to Crusades against infidels and violence against the Jews, to mass murder in pursuit of God's vengeance, to the imposition of a 'Christian' code on recalcitrant heathens, to intolerance and cruelty in pursuit of a 'higher' end, to the Inquisition, and to intrusion on private thoughts by torture, are all part of the West's Christian legacy. These discordant themes are still echoed among some Christian fundamentalists. By and large, though, for at least a century and a half, extremist intolerance has been excised from Christianity. It keeps popping up, however, in secular guises, in revolutionary terror, extreme nationalism, communism and Nazism, and in perversions of other religions. These guises, too, came largely from Christianity and the West.

Perversion, mutation and reformation

The original Jesus movement was down-market, revolutionary and driven by individual conversion. The number of Christians was small, though growing very fast.[24] They were dispersed in many towns of the central and eastern Mediterranean, and met, sometimes secretly, in small house-cult groups. The radical message of individual development, access to a personal God, and love, the predominant themes of the first two centuries, changed dramatically in the following two. After the Emperor Constantine's

---

23 John 8.21, 44.

24 The best guess is that there were considerably fewer than 10,000 Christians in 100 CE, and about 200,000 in 200 CE. Since the Roman population in 200 CE was about 60 million, the Christians comprised only 0.3 per cent of the total. On the other hand, the number was probably growing at a compound annual growth rate of 3–4 per cent up to 200 CE, and closer to 6 per cent in the following century. By 300 CE there may have been six million Christians in the Roman Empire, 10 per cent of the population.

conversion in 312, Christianity became perverted into a Roman imperial cult. Rome the political power spawned Rome the authoritarian church. Christian officials now integrated into the Roman elite, often becoming rich and powerful, building up an elaborate and centralized ecclesiastical hierarchy, with its own courts and punishments, to parallel and sometimes challenge the imperial ones. Competition between different Christian doctrines was abruptly terminated by the pronouncements of church councils. Dogma, and heresy, were defined. The persecuted became the persecutors. The simple Christian message, and the primal Christian spirit based on personal experience of God, became overlaid with elaborate theological rulings, refined to the point of incomprehensibility. The direct line to God was cut off. The Church became more important than its members.

When the Roman Empire fell – according to Edward Gibbon, the result of barbarism and religion – the Roman church assumed the reins of power. Yet the ideal, clearly recorded in the Gospels, would not go away. However craven and conformist Christianity appeared, there were always elements of soul searching, self-criticism, conscience, creative individuality, and attempts to re-establish a direct relationship with God. The ideals of personal responsibility and the importance of the inner life survived.

After about 1100, helped by interaction with Islamic scholars, Greek science and philosophy were rediscovered and developed further by new autonomous universities. The human spirit deepened, creativity soared and the gene of Christian individualization and personal freedom multiplied enormously.

In 1517, Martin Luther rebelled against the West's supreme religious and cultural authority, and re-defined Christianity. The Protestant Reformation restored the relationship between individual believers and God, cutting out the Church's role as middleman. Under 'the priesthood of all believers', each person again stood before God, responsible for his or her eternal salvation or damnation. Luther, once a monk, married a former nun and started a family. Chastity was out; holy matrimony was in.

John Calvin's austere religion carried personal responsibility a stage further. The Christian's worldly vocation and success became a leading indicator of spiritual status. Within a century of so, in Protestant countries, especially those touched by Calvinism, individual responsibility, individual self-expression and individual self-advancement through hard work and honesty became automatic impulses, no longer triggered by religion, but part and parcel of the individual's way of life and self-esteem.

The death of God

Because the West took science and rational investigation further than any other civilization – inspired largely by a Christian desire to celebrate and understand God's creation – it was also the first to move towards a secular society. One unintended consequence of the Reformation was the separation of science from religion.

Unwittingly, science constantly moved the focus from God to nature and humanity. Nicholas Copernicus (1473–1543) moved the earth from the centre of creation; it became just another planet. In the seventeenth and eighteenth centuries, God became a celestial watchmaker. Having wound up the universe, he left it to run by natural laws. Charles Darwin (1809–1882) saw humans, like other animals, as the product of evolution. Friedrich Nietzsche (1844–1900) announced that 'God is dead' – God used to exist but evolution had marched on. The breakthroughs of twentieth-century science made the belief that the universe was purposefully designed for human benefit seem quaint.

In the process, Western secular values have trumped Christian ones. A century's biblical scholarship has revealed the human origins of, and constant flux in, early Christian beliefs, questioning not only the belief that the whole Bible can be the infallible word of God, but also the miracles, the Virgin Birth, and even the idea that Jesus intended to found a religion.

Christianity is divided into a sophisticated and diffident elite, which has yet to reconcile the modern world with a reinterpretation of traditional tenets; and the evangelical movement, whose vitality requires denial of truths from science and biblical scholarship. The fundamentalists are winning. The broadminded, mainline Protestant denominations, and the liberal wing of the Catholics, have too little to say, and are losing members by the day; while the evangelicals' trade in certainties, and to a lesser extent the authoritarian Catholic tradition, are flourishing.

The division within Christianity can be seen as a microcosm of all the divisions in the West today. The centre does not hold. Many Christians loathe other Christians – as in the dispute over gay bishops – with a passion they cannot muster to advance Christianity itself. Meanwhile, cosmopolitan and advanced ideas, and their rich endowment for the benefit of humankind, stand undefended and unasserted, even by the intellectuals who believe them, for fear of seeming earnest or elitist. Ignorance and mumbo-jumbo are promoted; wisdom and knowledge willingly take a back seat.

The increasing secularization of Western society; the decline of belief in God, especially among intellectuals and social scientists; and the increasingly severe divisions within the Christian community, reflecting profound differences in world-view, are serious issues for the West. At first, God's eclipse did not destroy optimism, personal responsibility or belief in progress. In the last century, however, the decline of religion in the West has gone along with soaring levels of cynicism, nihilism, paganism, selfishness, depression, and suicide. In 1895, Lord Acton confidently asserted: 'Opinions alter, manners change, creeds rise and fall, but the moral law is written on tablets of eternity.' Eternity did not last long. In 1995, Jung Chang gave an opposite view: 'If you have no God, then your moral code is that of society. If society is turned upside down, so is your moral code.' As poet Robert Browning (1812–89) prophetically observed, we have moved 'from an age of faith diversified by doubt to an age of doubt diversified by faith'.

Yet, on closer inspection, God is not dead. Religion of all kinds still thrives. Nor is the key contrast between the presence or absence of a moral code. The pivotal issue is the kind of moral code the West embraces – whether it comes from the hellfire version of Christianity, with its sincere intolerance and condemnation; or from a version, mainly secularized, of Christianity's equally authentic innovations of personal responsibility, love and universal fraternity.

Christ rises again . . . but the wrong Christ?

The most actively Christian country is the United States, which is also the country most influenced by the Jewish heritage. These religions are, on the whole, intensely practical, exemplifying the Jewish–Christian breakthrough of individual self-help and self-improvement. Religion is personalized and non-sectarian. It is still true, as Anthony Trollope said in 1860, 'everyone is bound to have a religion, but it does not matter much what it is'.[25]

Since the 1980s, however, religious enthusiasm in America, although retaining much of its force for good, has been clouded by an increasingly intolerant and anti-intellectual spirit, closer to the fourth component of Christianity we have described than to the other three. In 1993, a Gallup poll reported 47 per cent of Americans agreeing that 'God created human beings pretty much in their present form at one time within the last 10,000 years or so' – the literal view of Genesis. Sixty-eight per cent of Americans approved of the Creationist dogma being taught in biology classes. In 1999, 39 per cent of Americans said they were 'born again Christians'. With the election and re-election of George W. Bush, fundamentalism has secured a hearing in the White House it has rarely had before.

If we look to the creative and positive inheritance from Christianity – personal responsibility, love as the engine of self-improvement,

---

25 Quoted in Samuel P. Huntington (2004) *Who Are We? America's Great Debate*, The Free Press, New York.

and the liberal spirit of equality, inclusion and social justice – then the legacy is thriving, but mainly outside the Church. It lies, most of all, in the rise and rise of the self-help movement. The roots of this Anglo-American phenomenon go back at least to Benjamin Franklin, who wrote between 1771 and 1790,[26] and to Samuel Smiles, a British doctor and radical journalist, who published *Self Help* in 1859. The tradition continued with such hugely influential bestsellers as Dale Carnegie's *How to Win Friends and Influence People* (1936), Napoleon Hill's *Think and Grow Rich* (1937), and Norman Vincent Peale's *The Power of Positive Thinking* (1952). Since 1980, the self-help market has exploded, with books by authors such as Anthony Robbins, Paulo Coelho, James Redfield, and Deepak Chopra each selling tens of millions.

The self-help movement exports well throughout the West, and to Latin America. It appeals right across the social and educational spectrum. What shines through is the spiritual dimension of most self-help bestsellers. Practical advice sits cheek-by-jowl with reflections on the nature of the universe and the individual's place in it. Although many self-help writers are Christians, religion is generally soft-pedalled, often completely absent. Yet, in their evangelical tone, the intense loyalty that many writers command, their relentless optimism that human nature can be improved, the emphasis on people tapping into celestial forces, their tolerance and inclusiveness, their propensity to import spiritual ideas from the East, their conquest of guilt, and their adherence to love and self-discipline as the principal motors of improvement, the modern self-help movement is closer to the original Jesus movement than any contemporary Church.

There is another, more universal reason why the spirit of Christianity is not dead. Christianity originated the idea that God took a deep interest in every human being and could live within every individual. This idea – later becoming expressed in the belief that

---

26 Franklin wrote three self-help books: *The Art of Virtue*, *The Way to Wealth* and *Autobiography*.

everybody possessed a unique, immortal 'soul' – is one of the most successful of all time, because it took root and became universal and ineradicable everywhere in the West. Today, the idea of the soul has been secularized to become the idea of the self.[27] If all humans have a self, an inner personality which makes them not machines, not merely part of society, but *individual people* – a belief so deeply ingrained within the West that it seems strange even to enunciate it – then they should all be treated with respect, they are all valuable, and they all have the potential to develop, deepen, and improve their personalities.

The idea of the soul, or the self, is impossible to divorce from *striving, self-development* and *self-responsibility*. If there is one single essence of Christianity, it is this, and it is one that has survived totally intact and with undiminished force in the West today, quite independent of religious belief. With the idea of the soul safely transmuted into the idea of the self, Christianity has permanently changed the nature of the West. Few can doubt that the change is, on the whole, hugely positive. In this sense, it does not matter what happens to the number or proportion of Christian believers in the West, because Christianity has done its work and, almost certainly, it cannot now be undone. The Nazis and the communists tried to deny the ideas of the soul and the self, and this partly explains our revulsion against their atrocities. Short of a calamity that dehumanizes us all, it is very unlikely that the idea of the self can ever now be extirpated from the West.

---

27 Of course, the 'self' no longer carries the automatic religious connotations of the 'soul', the idea of immortality, for example, not necessarily being part of the idea of the 'self'. But the self, like the soul, is a non-material, non-empirical, elusive concept – the greatest and most universal article of faith in the Western world, the foundation of our rich and humane civilization, and the one faith that the West cannot live without.

Conclusion

God is doing better than the churches.

The liberating spirit of early Christianity; its invention of the inner self; its stress on individualization, rejection of authority, and love in personal relationships; its demands for compassion and equality for the downtrodden; and its promotion of self-discipline and self-improvement, have had a determining influence on the whole of the West, making it not just more successful than other civilizations, but also, at least to Western judgement, far more pleasing. Christianity has burst the banks of the Church, even of all religion. A sense of responsibility derived from thinking for oneself, and emerging from one's own struggles in life, is likely to be deeper than one derived from obedience to authority, and, whatever one's beliefs, to be closer to the spirit of Jesus.

There is a darker sub-text. It lies in the missionary zeal and revolutionary extremism bequeathed to the West, and the world, by early Christians.[28] The deviant gene of Crusading aggression – backed by science, technology and the most potent economic and military systems ever seen – mightily powered the West, leading in the nineteenth century to world domination. In the first half of the twentieth century, this deviant gene – divorced from religion, but retaining true millenarian ruthlessness – nearly tore the West, and hence the world, apart. When reunited with religious fundamentalism, the gene of divisive intolerance remains a potent threat to the West, not just from outside, but more menacingly from within.

---

28 Such intolerance has generally been confined to Christianity and its cousin Islam. Eastern religions tend to be open to penetration by other ideas and feel little need to assert that there is one right way. Religious wars, endemic throughout Western and Middle Eastern history, have always been rare in Asia.

3 Optimism

From the dawn of Western civilization to the early years of the twentieth century, the history of the West was dominated by one idea and one reality – that of ever greater optimism about humanity, and confidence in our ability continually to improve the world. Optimism led to activism – actions designed to increase our understanding and control of the natural world. Optimism has always been pre-eminently a Western trait. As psychologist Richard Nisbett says:

> To the Asian, the world is a complex place . . . subject more to collective than to personal control. To the Westerner, the world is a relatively simple place . . . highly subject to personal control. Very different worlds indeed.[1]

The roots of optimism

Three intertwined beliefs lie at the heart of Western optimism. One is the *autonomy myth*[2] – people can be self-starting and autonomous, that they have the potential to take charge of their destiny, to shape the world around them for their own benefit. The second is the *goodness myth* – creation is ultimately good, and

---

1 Richard E. Nisbett (2003) *The Geography of Thought: How Asians and Westerners Think Differently . . . And Why*, Nicholas Brealey, London, p. 100.

2 In calling the three beliefs 'myths', we mean that they are powerful embodiments of unverifiable concepts; we are not using 'myth' in any pejorative sense.

humans, as part of God's creation, are basically good too, and can become better. The third is the *progress myth* – history is on the march, it has direction, that the present is better than the past and the future will be better than the present.

The three myths of optimism originated in the five or six centuries before Christ and in the first three centuries after his birth, in Jewish and Christian theology and Greek philosophy. The autonomy myth was most clearly enunciated by the Greeks, who placed the highest importance on reason and the mind, the *nous* or active intelligence. Greek philosophers argued that humans alone had minds, giving them the capacity to grasp truths about the universe. Minds were individual and linked to other minds and to divine intelligence. They were therefore restless and progressive, always developing, divine and eternal. People could learn more about the nature of reality through the exercise of reason, through logic, through mathematics, through drama, through exploration and architecture. The rest of nature was passive. People could – and should – be active, optimistic, questioning, creative and self-advancing. People could control their surroundings by learning the rules governing nature.

The Greeks subscribed to the goodness myth too. The cosmos was ordered and rational; the intelligent person could understand it, control it, and improve it. At the heart of Greek philosophy was the ideal of excellence, an elevated view of what humankind could achieve. Creation was not only good, but also getting better, through heroic exercise of the mind. Plato, with his idea of the soul, gave the clearest view of humanity's inherent or potential goodness. The soul, though trapped within the body and constrained by one's material nature, was precious to God, gave man access to God, and enabled one to attain virtue.

Greek philosophers also had a unique influence on the progress myth. Aristotle invented the idea of *potentiality* – the deepest reality was not *what is*, but *what will be*. Ultimate reality resided not in the beginning of things but in their *telos*, their end, that to which they aspire, their purpose and final form. This is a supremely optimistic world-view – implying that everything is working toward a better manifestation of the cosmos, planned by divine providence and abetted by human reason, which is cumulative and marching forward. What matters is what the world and people are *becoming* – what they will be when they reach their full potential.

At the same time, in a different way, Hebrew prophets also advanced the ideas of autonomy, goodness and progress. We saw in the previous chapter that Ezekiel (597–563 BCE) and other prophets called for individuals to take personal responsibility and exercise initiative and demonstrate mercy, social justice and love. The world's fate would be determined by human actions; the Hebrews saw progress as the hand of God in human history. At the end of time, a Messiah, a divine leader, would appear. History would reach its triumphal climax, and through the Hebrews, God would establish his kingdom to the ends of the earth, bringing joy and salvation to all humanity. Despite all that has happened to the Jews, in ancient, medieval and modern times, they never let go of their optimism, activism and mission to the whole world, leading to results far disproportionate to their numbers.

In fusing Greek and Jewish ideas, the early Christians took them to new heights of optimism and activism, adding their own millennial twist. To an extent never seen before, Jesus' followers moved to convert men and women, rich and poor, Jew and Greek, Roman and barbarian, slave and free, firing every individual Christian with the pressing need to lead good lives and 'save' those around them.

Within Christian theology, God's love and goodness are unimpeachable, and, through Christ, men and women are given access to the divine nature. After Christianity had become the official state religion of the Roman Empire, in the fourth century, Christian theologians had to contend with a highly influential and contrary view of the nature of good and evil. The fastest growing religion in the world was no longer Christianity, but Manichaeism, founded by a third-century Persian who taught that good and evil influences in the universe were perpetually at war; humankind was caught up in this struggle and could not escape the forces of evil.

This pessimistic religion undermined human activism and induced a fatalistic view of life and history – good could never gain the upper hand; there was no all-powerful and good God.

As violence engulfed the newly Christian Roman Empire, and it began to fall apart, Manichaeism posed a huge intellectual challenge to Christianity – the presence of evil and suffering was undeniable. An African, St Augustine of Hippo (born 354), rose to the challenge. He argued that all creation is good, and that humankind is God's greatest creation, since we have the ability freely to emulate God's goodness. In creating human free will, however, God necessarily had to allow us the liberty to choose either evil or good. All evil therefore results from the human misuse of free will. Evil is neither inevitable, nor inescapable, nor eternal. Ever since Augustine, this demanding but cheerful doctrine has remained at the heart of Christianity and of the West.

The myth of progress, too, was super-charged by Christianity. Though first-century Christian expectations of an imminent and glorious end to history had to be indefinitely postponed, the idea persisted that God's purpose is being worked out in history, through his new chosen people – Christians of all nations.

The retreat, resurgence and zenith of optimism

Though the three Western myths of optimism never withered or disappeared, they were muted or went underground from the time that the Roman Empire declined and disintegrated, until new stirrings of growth and civilization became progressively stronger after 1000. In between, economic decline and the emergence of the Roman church as society's most powerful institution discouraged and dampened ideas of autonomy, goodness and progress. As the Church grew more powerful, hierarchical, introverted and politically conservative, the pessimistic version of Christianity emerged. At a time of economic, cultural and psychological depression, the gloomy strain in medieval Christianity grew ever more influential, stressing the lethal threat posed by 'the world, the flesh and the devil'. The threat could only be countered by pious obedience to the Church; by rituals and relics; by seeking the protection of angels and saints, among whom the Virgin Mary grew ever more prominent; by developing an interior other-worldly religiosity; and, if possible, by retreat from the world.

After 1000, Europe attained a measure of political security. Economic growth, trade and population all began a hesitant upward curve; agriculture became more productive; trade in produce grew; and autonomous city-states emerged as islands of trade and relative freedom. Most important of all, contact with Islamic and Byzantine cultures enabled Europe in the twelfth and thirteenth centuries to rediscover the work of ancient Greek philosophers and scientists. Influenced by Aristotle and Plato, Thomas Aquinas (1225–74) declared that every person was created in the image of God and could participate, to some degree, in God's infinite creativity for good. Scholars such as Aquinas and William of Ockham (1295–1349) gave the West renewed and increasing confidence in human reason, scientific experimentation and intellectual freedom from ecclesiastical authority.

The rediscovery by Plutarch (born at the start of the fourteenth century) and his followers of the extraordinary depth and richness of Greek and Roman culture provided a new platform for optimism about humanity, its creativity and its greatness. The ancient literary classics were seen as enriching the human spirit and providing a new stream of insight about humanity's role in the cosmos comparable to that of Christianity itself. In the fifteenth century, Marsilio Ficino, Pico della Mirandola and other humanists reinterpreted Plato to argue that humans had a divine mission to control the visible universe by understanding its physical and mathematical laws. Ficino credited humanity with 'almost the same genius as the Author of the heavens'.

The new view of this potential was most clearly expressed in the Renaissance. As Richard Tarnas says:

Within the span of a single generation, Leonardo, Michelangelo, and Raphael produced their masterworks, Columbus discovered the New World, Luther . . . began the Reformation, and Copernicus . . . commenced the Scientific Revolution . . . Man was now capable of penetrating nature's secrets . . . [he] expanded the known world, discovered new continents, rounded the globe . . . music, tragedy and comedy, poetry, painting, architecture, and sculpture all achieved new levels of complexity and beauty.[3]

Renaissance man viewed himself as a co-creator alongside God. Western ideas, patterns of thinking, aspirations, drive and faith in the rationality of the universe and the power of man's imagination began to impose themselves on the world. From the fifteenth century, Westerners started a series of oceanic voyages which shrank the world, for the first time, into one global entity – within a century of Columbus' first voyage, Westerners had circumnavigated the world.

The seventeenth century was marked by an explosion of science, which for the first time discovered the basic physical laws of the universe, laying the foundations for the machine age, which in turn has transformed the world. Like the voyages, the Scientific Revolution was powered by Western optimism and exclusively executed by Europeans. From Columbus to Brunel to Einstein, one defining characteristic of the West is spontaneous action by individuals – the exercise of human initiative largely independently of existing organizations and hierarchies, the explorer mentality, the restless quest to find or build something different or better. The achievements of the West – for good and ill – have not, at the deepest level, been due to science or technology or the economic system. Rather, these enabling mechanisms are the *result* of something more fundamental: liberating ideas, experimentation, attitude, optimism and a very high opinion of humanity's potential and of a benevolent and rational deity.

---

3   Richard Tarnas (1991) *The Passion of the Western Mind*, Crown, New York.

Western science achieved so much because its ambition knew no bounds and because it was constantly directed toward practical ends to improve life on earth. Without this spirit, technology is not enough. The ancient Egyptians had steam-powered temple doors. The ancient Greeks had steam toys. But the idea of using steam power to make useful products came more than 2,000 years later, in eighteenth-century Britain. Centuries before the Scientific Revolution, Islamic society had the world's greatest science and technology. In 1400, before Europeans began sailing across oceans, China had a massive fleet, by far the largest in the world, comprising hundreds of ships and more than 20,000 sailors. There are, of course, particular reasons why Islamic technological innovation was interrupted, and why the Chinese in 1432 decided to dismantle their shipyards and stop sailing their ships.[4] But it is not coincidental that the West had an ideology of optimistic expansion based on a high view of human potential, and Islam and China did not.

The work of scientists such as Kepler, Copernicus, Galileo and Newton was both motivated by optimism and greatly reinforced by it. Science was a manifestation of man's potential, his reason and imagination. Science served a *purpose* – raising humanity's game, giving man control of nature and the universe so that he could improve his standing and add dignity and nobility to human life. 'The true and lawful end of the sciences,' Francis Bacon declared, 'is that human life be enriched by new discoveries and powers.'

French philosopher René Descartes (1596–1650) made human reason the supreme test of knowledge. For the first time in history, human happiness was thought to be the point of the universe. The poet Alexander Pope saw human nature following two complementary principles:

---

4 See Jared Diamond, 'How to get rich,' *Edge* 56, 7 June 1999 (www.edge.org/documents/archive/edge56), and Jared Diamond (1997) *Guns, Germs and Steel: A Short History of Everybody for the Last 13,000 Years*, Chatto & Windus, London.

Self-love and Reason to one end aspire,
Pain their aversion, Pleasure their desire . . .

Enlightenment thinkers in eighteenth-century Europe and
America were the greatest exponents of autonomy, human
goodness and perfectibility, and progress. Immanuel Kant identified the Enlightenment with human autonomy – the courage to
use one's own understanding, alone.

Enlightenment philosophers went even further than Descartes
in elevating the human mind, which they saw as separate from
and superior to the rest of nature. Denis Diderot (1713–84) highlighted the uniqueness of humankind in giving meaning to life: 'It
is the presence of man which makes the existence of being meaningful.'[5]

Freed from superstition, we could become more knowledgeable,
more ethical, more humane and more original. Historian Edward
Gibbon declared:

> We cannot be certain to what height the human species may
> aspire . . . We may therefore safely acquiesce in the pleasing con-
> clusion that every age of the world has increased, and still
> increases, the real wealth, the happiness, and perhaps the virtue,
> of the human race.[6]

The Romantic poets and writers of the early nineteenth century
took an even stronger view of the mind's potential. They saw it as
most powerful in the exercise of imagination, the ability to
transform the everyday into something special, to discern beyond
the world's surface level a deeper truth, to 'see into the life of
things', as Wordsworth wrote in *Tintern Abbey*. For the Romantics
– precursors of modern environmentalists – the relationship of the

---

5 Denis Diderot, *Encyclopédie*, p. 56. See www.tuna.uchicago.edu/homes/mark/
   ENC_Demo.
6 Edward Gibbon (1993) *The History of the Decline and Fall of the Roman
   Empire*, Vol. I, Everyman, London.

human mind and perception to the outside world was utterly transformed by the imagination's intensity.

One further development – economic growth – fuelled optimism. The expansion in trade from about 1450 to 1750, and the subsequent explosion of machine-based industry, was closely linked, both ways, to optimism and activism. The link between optimism and economic innovation is experimentation and the autonomy of traders and entrepreneurs. Optimism implies not being afraid to experiment. Economic growth requires innovation; innovation was possible in the West because the power to experiment and to diffuse successful new techniques and technologies was widely spread. Decentralization was essential; it required autonomous, optimistic entrepreneurs.[7] Many of the greatest economic innovators of the late eighteenth century, such as Benjamin Franklin, Josiah Wedgwood, Joseph Priestley and James Watt, were devotees of Enlightenment thinking and great protagonists of progress.

By the end of the nineteenth century, as growth in Western economies became undeniable, as new miracles of technology – the railways, cheap steel, electricity, gas, national postal systems, the telegraph, the telephone, canned food, photography, automobiles – emerged and mushroomed, and as the West's economic lead over the rest of the world became larger and larger, material evidence of progress was added to philosophical reflection as a major source of optimism. Whether they were industrialists or political agitators or intellectuals, whether conservatives, liberals, social democrats or communists, late nineteenth- and early twentieth-century opinion-formers were virtually unanimous in believing that modern Western industry had the potential to banish hunger and poverty from its society.

---

7 See Nathan Rosenberg and L. E. Birdzell, Jr (1986) *How the West Grew Rich: The Economic Transformation of the Industrial World*, Basic Books (Harper-Collins), New York.

The death of optimism

The roots of modern pessimism may be traced back at least as far as the 1760s, when English 'Gothic novels' revived grim supernatural images, portrayed egotistical heroes and heroines, and fractured the harmony of divine and human benevolence. Whether in the fantasies of German Romantics from the 1770s, the depravity of de Sade's fiction in the 1780s, or the mob-fuelled terror of the French Revolution, humanity's dark side, previously ignored or smothered by the flat idealism of the Enlightenment, erupted into full view. In the decades before 1914, the bombs of the Russian nihilists, the philosophy of Schopenhauer, the art of the early Expressionists, and the psychological explorations of Freud, combined to support a gloomy view of humanity's character and destiny. But nothing destroyed the optimistic illusions of the eighteenth and nineteenth centuries more completely and utterly than the events of 1914 to 1945.

Belief in man's autonomy, in his goodness and in the progress of Western civilization were crushed, for a generation and perhaps for ever, by a series of cataclysms and reactions to them – by the appalling nature and consequences of the Great War; by the growing belief that objectivity excluded the search for meaning; and by the perception, evident for example in Franz Kafka's prophetic novels of the mid-1920s, that people are not really free and self-determining, but are dominated and subdued by elusive, evil influences, at once terrifying, bureaucratic and beyond comprehension. Such horrific societies soon came to pass throughout Central and Eastern Europe, as Stalin and Hitler disfigured and dismantled Western civilization. Even in America and the few parts of Europe left untouched by states of hate, the 1930s were dominated by economic collapse and theories of the discontents of Western civilization, only partly staved off by the valiant efforts of optimist Franklin D. Roosevelt. Humankind's development had gone awry; it seemed, as Bertrand Russell said, that 'thought is the gateway to despair'.

From 1917 to 1989, the West's survival was in doubt, as communism and Nazism – both Western ideas, yet bitter and nearly terminal enemies of Western civilization – waxed and waned.

Even the end of the totalitarian nightmare and 60 years of prevalent peace and prosperity have not re-established the West's historic optimism. The picture today has two frames. Europeans, literary intellectuals, the media, popular culture and the bottom third of earners, incline towards pessimism; Americans, Australians, business people, scientists, political elites and the rich towards optimism. Fatalism's gravity is stronger.

The decline of optimism since 1900 can be related most of all to evidence, or apparent evidence, that the whole Western view of humankind, and in particular the prevailing view from 1700 to 1900, was substantially too generous. Man's autonomy and goodness, and belief in historical progress, had been implicitly called into question right at the start of the twentieth century, with the publication of Sigmund Freud's *The Interpretation of Dreams*. Half a century earlier, Karl Marx had claimed that man's freedom and autonomy were delusions. Now Freud appeared to supply the evidence. By inventing the idea of the unconscious, and by detailing the sexual obsessions that motivated even the most outwardly competent individuals and trapped them in habitual responses, Freud undermined the notion of human freedom. Psychological awareness opened up a Pandora's box of seething internal conflict, repression, alienation, guilt, shame and unending neurosis.

Freud had no doubts about the importance of his work and the shadow it cast. 'Humanity', he wrote, 'has in the course of time had to endure from the hands of science three great outrages upon its naïve self-love' – the discovery that the world is a speck in a vast universe rather than the centre of the heavens; the discovery that we were not uniquely created by God but descended from apes; and the discovery that our conscious minds do not tell us how we act but rather tell us a self-serving fairy tale.[8] Perhaps no single

---

8 Quoted in Steven Pinker (2002) *The Blank Slate: The Modern Denial of Human Nature*, Penguin, New York.

intellectual has changed Western thinking more profoundly, turning prevalent optimism into prevalent pessimism.

What Freud started, genetics, neo-Darwinian biology and the cognitive neuroscience of the last 50 years have completed. The discovery by Francis Crick and James Watson in 1953, that humans share the same basic DNA structure with all other plants and animals, upgraded the significance of genes. In 1976, the Oxford biologist Richard Dawkins presented a new twist on human autonomy. His hugely influential book, *The Selfish Gene*, saw the hereditary gene as the fundamental unit of selection and self-interest.[9] Modern neuroscience has shown that our minds are composed of intricate neural circuits for thinking, feeling and learning.

The new knowledge about genes and the mind has challenged two ideas that previously underpinned Western optimism about human nature. One idea, common throughout the eighteenth and nineteenth centuries, was that everyone's mind starts out as a 'blank slate', which can be filled in at will by parents, educators and society. We now know, however, that this idea is wrong.[10] Changing peoples' experiences can have some impact, but it cannot re-design their character. The other, much older idea supporting a sunny view of humanity was, as noted earlier, the idea of the soul, which had been pretty much unquestioned in the West since the triumph of Christianity. Twentieth-century neuroscientists looked in vain for the soul.

For intellectuals and ordinary citizens alike, psychoanalysis and neuroscience appeared to vindicate the gloomy view of human nature evident from the atrocities of the twentieth century and from the appalling wars that have raged somewhere in the world every day since 1939. Television and the press present unrelenting evidence of humanity's depravity. Even in the heart of the West, untouched since 1945 by major conflict, pessimists can find plenty

---

9   Richard Dawkins (1976, revised edition 1989) *The Selfish Gene*, Oxford University Press, Oxford.
10 See Pinker (2002).

of evidence that human nature is weak or rotten, as depression, narcissism, alcoholism, drug abuse, self-obsession and suicide have all soared, especially among young people, and as the chords of civility and community appear to have become severed by all-pervading materialism, greed and selfishness.

The only problem with this clear and widespread view – that science and twentieth-century experience vindicate pessimism – is that it is false. That is not to say that optimism is any more vindicated by the facts. It is just that the foundations of modern pessimism are a great deal shakier than they appear.

To an extent unappreciated by the general public, scientists and historians are now taking a very jaundiced view of Freud and his findings. In 1972, Sir Peter Medawar, the eminent British doctor and Nobel Prize winner, judged psychoanalysis to be 'one of the saddest and strangest of all landmarks in the history of twentieth century thought'.[11] The historian of ideas, Peter Watson, who presents a fair and balanced account of twentieth-century thought, finds Freud's legacy deeply flawed: Freudian novels, paintings and operas, says Watson, 'have helped to popularize and legitimize a certain view of human nature, one that is, all evidence to the contrary lacking, wrong'.[12] Watson says that Freud's 'research' is now largely discredited and that most of his ideas are entirely unscientific, 'on a par with belief in flying saucers'.

Neuroscience and neo-Darwinian biology cannot be dismissed this way. Yet their implications need not be as pessimistic as first thought. 'The passing of the Blank Slate', says Steven Pinker, 'is less disquieting, and in some ways less revolutionary, than it at first appears . . . The megalomania of genes does not mean that benevolence and cooperation cannot evolve, any more than the law of gravity proves that flight cannot evolve.'

---

11 Peter B. Medawar (1972) *The Hope of Progress*, Methuen, London, p. 68.
12 Peter Watson (2000) *A Terrible Beauty: The People and Ideas that Shaped the Modern Mind – A History*, Weidenfeld & Nicolson, London.

The optimists strike back

The crucial ground for optimists and pessimists is the conception of human nature. Did twentieth-century science really justify a much gloomier view of humans? Our conclusion so far is: not really. Freudian ideas have been influential, but are not justified by the evidence. The importance of genetic influences on humanity, and the retreat of the 'blank slate', argue strongly against the perfectibility of man, yet in a way they heighten rather than diminish the importance of our free will, and the nobility of civilization achieved by humanity in transcending our purely animal and physical influences.

In 1996, Matt Ridley's book, *The Origins of Virtue*, interpreted the latest evidence from biology and game theory to support an optimistic view of humanity and society. He argued that society is a product of our genes *and* our non-genetic evolution. Humans are unique because we organize ourselves into large groups, with complex inter-relationships between individuals – and because we cooperate in a fundamentally different way from other animals: 'The human brain is not just better than that of other animals; it is different . . . it [is able to] exploit reciprocity, to trade favours and to reap the benefits of social living.'[13] Ridley links this to the invention of trade, which, he says,

> . . . represents one of the very few moments in evolution when *Homo Sapiens* stumbled on some competitive ecological advantage over other species that was truly unique. There is simply no other animal that exploits the law of comparative advantage between groups.

The importance of trade and cooperation can be graphically illustrated by contrasting native Tasmanians and native Aboriginal

---

13 Matt Ridley (1996) *The Origins of Virtue*, Penguin, New York.

Australians. When Europeans landed in Tasmania in 1842, they found the most primitive society in the world at that time. Native Tasmanians couldn't light a fire. They didn't have bone tools or axes with handles or boomerangs. They couldn't fish or make warm clothing. The Aborigines could do all these things. Isolated groups such as the Tasmanians suffer because most societies get their ideas and innovations from outside, through trade in goods and ideas. Human society progresses through trade, specialization and inter-group cooperation.

After 1970, mathematicians developed game theory using computers, comparing the outcome of players who cooperate with each other against those who pursue their own selfish interests. One concept that game theory used was the 'prisoner's dilemma', where two criminals, locked up in separate rooms, can escape punishment only if they both independently refuse to betray each other. Given a deal of immunity or a light sentence if they implicate the other prisoner, both parties will selfishly choose that route. This seemed to suggest, in classic modern style, following Marx, Freud and much recent history, that conflict was endemic to society and that cooperation was bound to be dominated by selfishness. But in 1979, political scientist Robert Axelrod organized two tournaments, inviting people to submit rival computer programs to play the prisoner's dilemma game 200 times against each other program entered, against itself, and against a random program. Each time, out of a total of 76 submissions, the same program won. Called 'Tit-for-Tat', and devised by Canadian political scientist Anatol Rapoport, it began by cooperating and then did the same as the other player did the previous time. Alexrod explained why 'Tit-for-Tat' won:

> What accounts for Tit-for-Tat's robust success is its combination of being nice, forgiving, and clear. Its niceness prevents it from getting into unnecessary trouble. Its retaliation discourages the other side from persisting whenever defection is tried. Its forgiveness helps to restore mutual co-operation. And its clarity

makes it intelligible to the other player, thereby eliciting long-term co-operation.[14]

A further case for optimism was made in 2000 by neurobiologist Kenan Malik.[15] He says that humankind has escaped from the bondage of the physical and the biological into social existence. Humans share 98 per cent of their genes with chimpanzees, yet have achieved a quite different existence through language, self-awareness, imagination and the use of symbols. 'Humans', he argues, 'are aware of themselves as agents, and of the world towards which their agency is directed.' Humans achieve more than the sum of individual actions by cooperating in society. We are not just physical beings, but social beings too. 'The brain may well be a machine. The mind is not.' What distinguishes the mind is that, unlike the brain, it does not belong purely to the individual. The mind is influenced by, and influences, other minds; it is in ideas and relationships that humans are qualitatively different from other animals.

Humans change the world; they change cultures rather than simply accept them. Humans create tools – language, concepts, technology – that go beyond the human inheritance from natural selection. They depend fundamentally on relationships, empathy, cooperation and collaboration.

Writers such as Ridley and Malik draw us back to the miracles that civilization has achieved, through human cooperation and creativity. Our greater understanding of what we are like has, perhaps, three useful implications. One is that there is an enormous range of human behaviour. The second is that, over the long haul, human cooperation, based on ever more complex societies and greater interdependence, has enabled humans to thrive and multiply. The third inference is that cooperation does

14 Robert Axelrod (1984) *The Evolution of Co-operation*, Basic Books, New York.
15 Kenan Malik (2000) *Man, Beast and Zombie: What Science Can and Cannot Tell Us About Human Nature*, Weidenfeld & Nicolson, London.

not work automatically, but needs to be stimulated by conventions that encourage cooperation and discourage selfishness.

Once the pessimistic view of human nature is sidelined, there are few other objective grounds for pessimism. The perception that the twentieth century was uniquely bloody is not correct. In various primitive societies, the percentage of male deaths caused by warfare ranged from 10 to 60. The equivalent percentage for the West in the last century, including deaths from two world wars, was just 2 per cent.[16] Nor does increasing media attention to warfare mean that it is getting worse. A recent University of Maryland study showed that, compared to 15 years ago, the frequency and intensity of war has declined by more than half.[17]

There are, however, two final developments we should highlight which, while not necessarily providing a justification for increased pessimism, certainly help to explain it. One, well noted and understood, is the 'creative destruction' wrought by the dismantling of controlled capitalism – by deregulation, privatization, reduction of import barriers, and other manifestations of increasingly free and anarchic markets. Overall wealth is increasing, but so too are income disparities and personal insecurity.

The second development is less obvious and more important. 'In the twentieth century,' Gertrude Stein said, 'nothing is in agreement with anything else.' We have moved from an integrated society toward a much more fragmented, plural society. Karl Marx, along with almost every other nineteenth-century thinker, believed that the different institutions of society – political, economic, religious, social, and more broadly intellectual – naturally reinforced each other. What Marx could not imagine is what the West now manifests – a world where business, the arts, the Church, the media, the political classes, scientists, literary intellectuals and

---

16 Data from Pinker (2002), p. 57.
17 Quoted in 'Trends in high places' by Stein Ringen, *Financial Times* magazine, 23 July 2005, p. 23. If we find this surprising, it indicates how far contemporary pessimism has distorted our perceptions.

other professional groups, and groups affiliated by ethnic or sub-
cultural identities, may be at odds with some or all of the other
groups, or else may be indifferent to them, with varying degrees of
mutual toleration and respect.

Unity and consensus are more difficult today because different
parts of modern life have their own autonomy and distinctive
mores. The added complexity and differentiation of society
probably tend to increase cultural richness, wealth, knowledge and
personal freedom; but they also tend to decrease a sense of our
common identity and interests. Optimism and confidence in
society may well therefore decline even if objective indicators of
well-being and progress are trending up. If we add in the dramatic
decline, in the past half-century, of public confidence and trust in
government – hitherto, along with historians, the main sustainers
of society's necessary myths about itself and its virtues – we can see
how proliferating pessimism may coexist with increasing social
progress.

Conclusion

The West's success has been substantially driven by optimism.
Now the roots of optimism appear to have shrivelled.

It is better to be realistic than to deceive ourselves; yet whatever
the facts, there is a huge spectrum of optimism or pessimism
through which individuals and civilizations may choose to
interpret reality. The world exists in our minds; our attitude to the
world feeds our actions and strongly influences our degree of
success. Whether a civilization is active or passive, self-confident or
self-critical, united or divided, will to a large extent determine its
trajectory. Without self-esteem, an individual can do little constructive. The same is true of societies and civilizations.

The greatest challenge to optimism in the past 100 to 150 years
was a new downbeat view of humanity, apparently derived from
discoveries in biology and psychology. There is no denying the

extent to which we tend to take a darker view of humanity. Yet there is nothing in modern science that requires such despair. We have lost belief in the blank slate, in human perfectibility. But we also have a clearer and stronger view of humanity's unique differences from other animals, of the glory of the mind, of the reality of free will, of our ability to evolve through shared language, ideas and our control of nature, and of the achievements of ever more complex, interdependent and cooperative societies.

The inherent tendency of modern Western civilization is to decentralize, fragment and dissolve the bonds that used to unite more homogeneous societies. The price of progress may be to perceive less evidence of it. The big picture is harder to see, and harder still to appreciate to the fullest justifiable extent.

If 'realistic optimism' makes us happier and is a condition for the advance of our civilization, then the West is severely challenged. We are not only victims of our own success; we also cannot count on it continuing. We have nothing to be pessimistic about but pessimism itself. Yet to view our civilization and our humanity in a gentler and more positive light runs counter not just to our prevailing prejudices, but also to centrifugal social trends which are still accelerating. It would take a whole new intellectual and practical movement to swing the West back to optimism. There is no sign of such a shift on the horizon. Although there are no compelling reasons for gloom, and many practical reasons to look on the bright side, it is difficult to be optimistic about the future of optimism.

4   Science

More than any of the other five success factors, the triumph of science explains the West's current enormous lead over other civilizations in technology, innovation, living standards and military might. Scientific achievement since 1900 has been more far reaching in both intellectual and practical terms than at any other time, crowning six centuries of amazing discoveries about nature and the universe. The achievements and discoveries were, and continue to be, overwhelmingly Western.

Knowing these facts, a visiting Martian might imagine that science would be worshipped by many or most Westerners, and that its standing would never have been higher. At times – perhaps during the night of 20/21 July 1969, when Neil Armstrong stepped onto the moon – this may have been fleetingly true. But since the 1920s, and more particularly since 1970, Western misgivings about science have greatly increased. The last 30 years have seen, from within the heart of the West, an astonishingly vehement and varied series of attacks on science, assaults coming from left and right, from intellectuals and anti-intellectuals, from the media and angry protesters, from Bible-bashers and New Age gurus. Westerners appear to have lost faith in reason and science.

In this chapter, we pose and answer two curiously under-debated questions. *Why* has science in its heyday, and for the past 600 years, been virtually a Western monopoly? And what explains the decline in the standing of science at the time of its greatest triumph? It turns out, intriguingly, that the answer to both questions is the same.

And it bodes ill for Western civilization.

The rise of science

What is science? Depending on the definition, the West is either the most developed scientific civilization, but resting importantly on previous leading scientific civilizations, or else the West is the first and only scientific civilization.

Anthropologist Jared Diamond says 'science is often misrepresented as "the body of knowledge acquired by performing replicated controlled experiments in the laboratory". Actually, science is something much broader: the acquisition of reliable knowledge about the world.'[1]

If we take this broad definition, the West was not the first scientific civilization. In the sixth century BCE, the Ionian Greeks turned their backs on magic and, some historians claim, founded natural science. The Ionians said that human reason, guided by rigorous observation of the facts, could discover the nature of reality. Truth did not exist in a ghostly heavenly world, but in the observable world of human experience. Some Greeks held that by excluding mythological and supernatural explanations of the cosmos, natural phenomena could be understood in physical and mathematical terms. Knowledge, they said, is partial and fallible and should always be revised as new evidence and explanations emerge.

As is well known, Greek scholars made huge progress in mathematics and in philosophy. But the idea of gaining knowledge through observation and experimentation never took firm root. Socrates and Plato derided astronomical observation – Socrates called it 'a waste of time'. Greek progress toward science was hindered by the view propounded by Zeno (490–430 BCE), and almost universally accepted, that the cosmos operated in a personalized way, not according to natural laws. Aristotle said that the stars moved in circles because they liked to move this way. Stones

---

1 Jared Diamond (2005) *Collapse: How Societies Choose to Fail or Survive*, Penguin, New York.

fell to earth because they loved the centre of the world. It is not surprising that physics based on such 'explanations' failed to make much headway. Summarizing the views of many historians of science, Professor Rodney Stark says of the ancient Greeks, 'in the end, all they achieved were non-empirical, even anti-empirical, speculative philosophies, anti-theoretical collections of facts, and isolated crafts and technologies – they never broke through to real science'.[2]

After the fall of the Roman Empire, Islamic civilization became militarily, culturally and scientifically pre-eminent in Europe. It was under the umbrella of Islam, from the mid-tenth to the mid-thirteenth centuries, that European civilization first began to emerge from the so-called Dark Ages. When Christian Europe had lost nearly all Greek learning, it was known and treasured throughout Islam. The beautiful Islamic cities of Spain – Seville, Granada and Córdoba – were magnets for scholars of all faiths; Muslims, Jews and Christians collaborated to their great mutual benefit. Through the agency of Arab scholars, the West gained its modern numerals, rediscovered the writings of ancient Greek scientists, advanced in astronomy, and gained new learning from Persia, India, and particularly China, the only civilization to equal Islam for its science and technology.[3]

Nonetheless, Islamic science, like that of the ancient Greeks on which it was predicated, had serious limitations. Caesar E. Farah, the distinguished and devout Muslim historian, explains why: 'The early Muslim thinkers took up philosophy where the Greeks left off . . . in Aristotle the Muslim thinkers found the great guide . . . Muslim philosophy . . . in subsequent centuries merely chose

---

2 Rodney Stark (2003) *For the Glory of God: How Monotheism Led to Reformations, Science, Witch-Hunts, and the End of Slavery*, Princeton University Press, Princeton.

3 Chinese civilization had always outdistanced that of Greece and Rome in terms of technology, though the Chinese genius was for practical invention rather than scientific speculation or investigation.

to *continue* in this vein and to enlarge Aristotle rather than to innovate.'[4]

Meanwhile, for all their lack of Greek texts, the European 'barbarians' of the 'Dark Ages' made remarkable progress, not in science but certainly in technology. In 732 Charles Martel and a Frankish army routed the Muslim Saracens by deploying knights in full armour, using stirrups and the Norman saddle for the first time, enabling the knights to stay on their horses while lancing the Saracens. Over the next five centuries, Europeans invented machinery, historian Jean Gimpel says, 'on a scale no civilization had previously known.'[5] The list of innovations could stretch to more than a page: it included eyeglasses, camshafts, the compass, mechanical clocks, water mills, water wheels and gunpowder.[6]

From the eleventh century, European science began to catch up with and, by the end of the thirteenth century, surpass that of Islam and China. Robert Grosseteste (1186–1253), Bishop of Lincoln and Chancellor of Oxford University, originated the systematic method of scientific experimentation.[7] The invention of the mechanical clock in the 1270s led to a new precision in scientific measurement.

The 'Scholastics' – Christian monks, including the famous innovators Thomas Aquinas (1225–74), William of Ockham (1295–1349), Jean Buridan (1300–58), Nicholas d'Oresme (1325–82), and Albert of Saxony (1316–90) – invented the

---

4 Caesar E. Farah (1994) *Islam: Beliefs and Observances*, Barron's, Hauppauge, New York. Italics in the original.

5 Jean Gimpel (1976) *The Medieval Machine: The Industrial Revolution of the Middle Ages*, Penguin, New York.

6 The Chinese invented explosive powder to make fireworks; Europeans used it for gunpowder, so that by 1325 cannon existed all over Western Europe, and nowhere else.

7 *Ad hoc* experiments had been conducted by the empiricists in Alexandria, the Han age Chinese, and scientists in ninth-century Baghdad, but Grosseteste was the first to insist on the importance of the scientific *method*, and to propose the formulation of hypotheses to be precisely tested through experiments.

university,[8] replaced abstract speculation with empirical observation, sought the simplest and most parsimonious explanations for scientific hypotheses, and took experimentation, mathematics and physics to new heights.

The Scholastics' sophistication can be gauged by the way they grappled with concepts such as natural law, and the rotation of the earth round the sun. For example, Jean Buridan, rector of the University of Paris, first explored the hypothesis that the earth rotates on its axis, creating the illusion that the sun and the moon rise and set. Buridan also originated an early version of the theory of inertia and of the idea that God created the world and then left it to run according to natural laws. It could be argued, said Buridan,

> . . . that God, when He created the world, moved each of the celestial orbs as He pleased, in moving them He impressed upon them impetuses which moved them without His having to move them any more . . . And these impetuses which He impressed in the celestial bodies were not decreased nor corrupted afterwards . . . Nor was there resistance which could be corruptive or repressive of that impetus.[9]

Albert of Saxony, a later fourteenth-century rector of the University of Paris, even anticipated, by nearly three centuries, Newton's First Law of Motion: '. . . the First Cause created the celestial orbs and impressed one such motive quality on each of them, which moves the orb'. The stars continued to move in their orbits because there is no resistance in space and hence no force 'towards any opposite motion.'[10]

---

8   Bologna and Paris were first, around 1150, followed by Oxford and Cambridge around 1200, and more than a score of others, all in European cities, by 1300.
9   Quoted by Rodney Stark (2003), based on Marshall Clagett (1961) *The Science of Mechanics in the Middle Ages*, University of Wisconsin Press, Madison, p. 536.
10 Stark (2003), based on Edward Grant (1994) *Planets, Stars and Orbs: The Medieval Cosmos, 1200–1687*, Cambridge University Press, Cambridge, p. 550. The original source was Albert of Saxony (1493) *Physics*, Padua, a book which must have been known to Copernicus, who studied at Padua University shortly after its publication.

The Renaissance, which started around the second half of the fifteenth century, grew out of the fertile intellectual soil of medieval Europe. The half-decade from 1450 to 1455 saw the birth of Columbus and Leonardo, Gutenberg's invention of the printing press, and the migration of Greek scholars to Italy after the fall of Constantinople. Between 1468 and 1488 came the neo-Platonic revival of the Academy at Florence, Pico della Mirandola's matchless *Oration on the Dignity of Man*, and the births of Castiglione, Copernicus, Dürer, Giorgione, Luther, Magellan, Michelangelo, More, Pizarro and Raphael. Accomplishment in drawing and painting, such as the geometrical measurement of space, perspective and anatomical realism, were important spurs to later advances in medical and technical science. Leonardo, scientist as much as artist, laid down the three principles of modern science – empiricism, mathematics and mechanics.

The whole modern world rests upon one insight, foreshadowed by Buridan, Albert of Saxony, Leonardo and Copernicus, and explored and vindicated between 1609 and 1687 by Kepler and Newton – that the earth and the heavens are governed by a few universal, physical, mechanical and mathematical laws. In 1609, by using masses of astronomical data, Kepler proved that the earth moved round the sun and not the other way round. The same year, Galileo, using his own new powerful telescope, revealed innumerable new stars and a much vaster universe than previously envisaged. In 1687, Isaac Newton made perhaps the greatest intellectual breakthrough of all time – that four physical laws (three laws of motion, and the theory of universal gravitation) could explain everything previously known and observed about heavenly and earthly movements. This was the first convincing scientific theory of the entire solar system. No longer were the heavens mysterious or beyond human reason. Gravity explained why apples fall off trees and how the planets were held in place; mathematics elucidated every piece of data about physical movement. Human reason had at last penetrated the mysteries of the heavens. Newton's discovery gave tremendous confidence to all subsequent scientists, philosophers and engineers – everything made sense, everything fitted together, everything was mechanical, and everything could be investigated, predicted, managed and improved by science.

Why is science pre-eminently Western?

Rodney Stark defines science as 'a *method* utilized in *organized* efforts to formulate *explanations* of nature, always subject to modifications and corrections through *systematic observations* . . . science consists of two components: *theory* and *research*'. This definition enables him to conclude that 'science arose only once in history – in medieval Europe'.[11] The historian Edward Grant places the date of science's emergence slightly later but agrees it was a European invention: 'It is indisputable that modern science emerged in the seventeenth century in Western Europe and nowhere else.'[12]

A broader definition of science such as that proposed by Jared Diamond – 'the acquisition of reliable knowledge about the world' – would highlight the pioneering work of the ancient Greek, Islamic and Chinese civilizations.

The definition of science is not crucial. Every historian agrees that, some time between the thirteenth and the fifteenth centuries, Western Europe pulled well ahead of the rest of the world in science and technology, a lead consolidated in the next 200 years and never since challenged. A hundred years ago, Max Weber confidently asserted that 'only in the West does science exist at a stage of development which we recognize as valid today.'[13] In 2000, Peter

---

11 Stark (2003), pp. 124, 197.

12 Edward Grant (1996) *The Foundations of Modern Science in the Middle Ages: Their Religious, Institutional, and Intellectual Contexts*, Cambridge University Press, Cambridge, p. 168.

13 Max Weber (1985) *The Protestant Ethic and the Spirit of Capitalism*, Unwin, Hemel Hempstead.

Watson, writing a history of ideas, wrote that '. . . in the twentieth century, the non-Western cultures have produced no body of work that can compare to the ideas of the West . . . Whatever list you care to make of twentieth century innovations . . . it is almost entirely Western.'[14]

It is plain that the West was the first and only civilization fully to develop science, and that the priority the West gave to science enabled it to change the nature of the economy and society, to create general prosperity within the West, to achieve technological miracles of which earlier ages could not even have conceived, and to conquer whole continents. The importance of Western science is not in doubt, and whether it arose uniquely or to an unusual degree is not material. The more interesting question is *why* science is pre-eminently Western.

Science and God

In 1925, the mathematician Alfred North Whitehead first proposed the hypothesis, now widely accepted, that the inspiration for science derived 'from the medieval insistence on the rationality of God, conceived as with the personal energy of Jehovah [the Jewish God] and with the rationality of a Greek philosopher. Every detail was supervised and ordered: the search into nature could only result in the vindication of the faith in rationality.'[15]

During the time that science made its greatest strides, in medieval and early modern Western Europe, scholars believed that the secrets of the universe could be unravelled because they had been implanted by a reliable and all-powerful creator-God who had written nature's rules in a dependable way. Confidence that the universe was rational and consistent was essential for modern science; and that belief rested absolutely on belief that God was

14 Watson (2000).
15 Alfred North Whitehead (1967) *Science and the Modern World*, The Free Press, New York.

omnipotent, rational and consistent. God was perfect. His creation must therefore be perfect, and work in accordance with unchanging principles. Trust that there was a logical and consistent answer motivated scientists to find it. In the Middle Ages, this belief in the nature of God and the universe was unique to Christianity. From the thirteenth to the seventeenth centuries, virtually every important Western scientist was a devout Christian.

For most non-Christian religions, there is no rational Creator – the universe is inexplicable, capricious, unpredictable. The ancient Greeks, as we have seen, believed that objects such as stones or stars had their own motives. Islam did believe in one God, but Allah was thought to be an activist and sometimes inconsistent God, doing as he pleased, sustaining the world daily through his will. There was no parallel to the European sense of natural law immutably established by the Creator. As for Chinese intellectuals following the Tao, they did not believe that the world was created at all; it was eternal. The supernatural was an essence – inaccessible, impersonal, subtle, complex, and paradoxical. There was no impetus toward empirical science because there was no concept of a logical universe.[16]

The Christian view of God was a necessary condition for the take-off of modern science. Nonetheless, Christian theology – which had existed in all essentials for more than 1,000 years before science took off – is clearly not a sufficient explanation. Two other factors were essential: intellectual progress leading to a new view of humanity; and economic growth, which in turn importantly depended on progress towards freedom.

---

16 Oswald Spengler contrasted the European scientific method which 'from the earliest Gothic days, thrusts itself upon Nature, with the firm resolve to *be its master* . . . the Western [scientist] strives to *direct* the world according to his will'. With Chinese culture: '. . . the Chinese did not wrest, but *wheedled*, things out of Nature'. Oswald Spengler (1991), p. 410.

Science and humanity

In Chapter 3 we saw that the spirit of optimism underlying Western civilization propelled the civilization of the high Middle Ages, the Renaissance and the Enlightenment. Optimism implied a high degree of confidence in God's power and goodness, but from the fourteenth century Western optimism also embodied a very high view of humanity as God's supreme creation. In 1486, the 23-year-old Pico della Mirandola published his celebrated *Oration on the Dignity of Man*, where God tells Adam that '. . . I have set you at the center of the world . . . we have made you neither heavenly nor earthly, neither mortal nor immortal, so that . . . you may fashion yourself in whatever form you shall prefer'.[17] The Renaissance thinkers believed that there were no limits to the power of human imagination, that God wanted humankind to share in the process of creation through new discoveries in art and science. This positive and elevated view of human nature was peculiar to Western Europe at the time of science's greatest advance. Humanism was to grow stronger and stronger in European–American intellectual circles in the eighteenth and nineteenth centuries; even then it had no comparable echo outside the West.

Science and growth

Does science lead to economic growth, or does growth lead to science? The answer is that initially growth helped to lead to science; but in the last three centuries science has been one of the main causes of growth.

As we shall probe in the next two chapters, there was a unique development in Europe in the centuries after the year 1000 – the expansion and slow transformation of the European economies.

---

17 Tarnas (1991).

A virtuous circle linked three important trends: the proliferation of European trade; the growth in the number, wealth and political power of new, autonomous city-states; and the accelerating invention of new technologies. Scientific discoveries, in these centuries, appear to have been more the result than the cause of economic and political progress.

The first new technology to benefit European commerce substantially was the introduction of the three-mast ship in the mid to late fifteenth century, dramatically lowering transportation costs and boosting trade. With this exception, it was not for another two or three centuries that science and technology had a decisive impact on the Western economy. By the fifteenth century European science was much more advanced than anywhere else, and by the seventeenth century it was totally dominant; but it was not until the eighteenth and nineteenth centuries that the West's scientific hegemony translated into economic hegemony.

The richer and more complex European society engendered by trade and city-states contributed to the development of science in three ways. First, the economic surplus made it possible to devote more resources to intellectual and scientific activity: universities and colleges, for example, were increasingly funded and in some cases established by wealthy merchants. Second, economic expansion and increased wealth contributed to the spirit of discovery and optimism. Third, political power was increasingly fragmented. One key reason why science and the spirit of exploration triumphed in medieval Europe, and did not triumph in Islamic and Chinese societies at the same time, is that Europe was much more decentralized.

In 1432 a new Chinese emperor decided that the risk of cultural contamination from outside exceeded the benefits of trade. China's massive fleet of ships, many times larger than that of any other civilization, was scuttled and China's shipyards were dismantled, once and for all. In 1551, the Chinese emperor made it illegal even to *sail* a ship with several masts, and it was not until 1851 that a Chinese ship ever again docked in a European port. China's political centralization forfeited its clear lead in marine technology. Set off that vignette with Christopher Columbus' long-drawn-out attempts to secure finance for his transoceanic voyage from Europe in 1492. Columbus raised backing for his venture only at the sixth attempt – he was able to set sail only because of Europe's political fragmentation, which meant that there were dozens of heads of state to whom he could appeal.[18] As for Islam, the authorities effectively banned the printing press for fear of sacrilege, and there were no political enclaves within which new ideas could be protected.[19]

To summarize, science arose fully in Western Europe between the thirteenth and seventeenth centuries. A necessary condition for the full emergence of science was belief in one all-powerful God, whose perfect creation awaited rational, scientific explanation. This condition was fulfilled by Christianity but not by other religions. Still, it took Christians over 1,000 years to get round to inventing modern science. Intellectual progress from around the year 1000, and the recovery and enhancement of Greek humanism, were critical catalysts for science's take-off. Technological innovation was also important. So too was economic recovery and growth in Europe after 1000, which uniquely depended on the expansion and clout of more than 20 important city-states run by free burghers. Growth allowed universities to be founded and endowed and, along with a new view of the dignity of man, reinforced the spirit of optimism which pervaded the high Middle Ages and post-Renaissance Europe.

The discovery of America and successful European settlements there reinforced economic growth, intellectual progress, optimism and commitment to glorify God by full penetration of the universe's riddles. From the eighteenth century, breakthroughs in technology, loosely linked to scientific insights, led to unprecedented and automatic economic growth, based initially on the

---

18 This point is made forcibly in Jared Diamond in 'How to get rich', *Edge* 56, 7 June 1999. See also Diamond (1997).

19 See David Landes (1999) *The Wealth and Poverty of Nations: Why Some Are So Rich and Some So Poor*, Abacus, London.

steam engine, then on all other kinds of machines, and, from the nineteenth century to the present day, on fundamental scientific principles and research, and on the regimentation, and later the liberation, of people working in industry.[20]

From 1750, history broke its previous pattern; humanity mastered nature and built a new civilization. From then to now, the theoretical and practical achievements of science, the numbers and proportion of the population engaged in knowledge-based work, the economy, cities and urban civilization, technological innovation, living standards throughout society, and military, naval and latterly nuclear force, all grew and grew and grew, with no end in sight. All this was based on science and knowledge. Science and knowledge, in turn, were based on Christianity, optimism, humanism, liberty and economic growth. It was the Western commitment to control nature, the conviction that God's creation was rational, and the penchant for simple and elegant explanations that powered science and human mastery of the world.

This is not the end of the story. In the twentieth century, something strange and fateful happened to science, the pre-eminent engine of Western confidence and dominance.

What went wrong?

In 1900, the status of science had never been higher. But over the next hundred years, science faced two huge sets of challenges, one internal and theoretical, related to what scientists discovered and thought; and one external, related to a much more critical view of science from the rest of society.

The theoretical problem was that the Newtonian universe broke down. Advances in physics – in quantum mechanics and relativity – apparently revealed a baffling and inscrutable universe, ruled by mystery, uncertainty and chance.

---

20 These themes are explored in the next chapter.

In 1912–13, the great Danish physicist Niels Bohr (1885–1962), building on the work of New Zealander Ernest Rutherford (1871–1937), constructed a new view of the micro-world, of the smallest pieces of matter. Rutherford had developed a model of atoms as miniature solar systems, with a tiny nucleus of protons and neutrons orbited by tinier electrons. Bohr guessed that electrons radiated light when they changed orbit, and that they changed position instantly, passing from one position to another not adjacent to it, without physically passing through the intervening space. Electrons appeared to make these 'quantum jumps' entirely at random.

The German physicist Werner Heisenberg demonstrated in 1927 that uncertainty lies at the heart of the micro-world. It was impossible to measure *both* where an electron is, *and* its momentum. Heisenberg's 'uncertainty principle' showed that measurements of atoms and electrons were approximate and perhaps illusory. The idea that there is a 'real' world ruled by cause and effect, said Heisenberg, was 'useless and meaningless'.

The same year, Bohr showed that light is simultaneously like a wave and like a particle. When scientists observed a photon with a particle detector, they noted a particle. But if they looked at the same photon with a wave detector, they saw a wave. Light, said Bohr, is both a wave and a particle; both descriptions complement each other. This kind of thinking undermined centuries of 'either/or' scientific procedure. Science became fuzzy.

'Quantum mechanics', says Professor Martin Rees, Britain's Astronomer Royal, 'surpasses any other conceptual breakthrough in the breadth of its scientific ramifications, and in the jolt its counterintuitive consequences gave to our view of nature.' Quantum mechanics was so strange and subversive that it offended Albert Einstein, who dubbed it 'the delusions of an exceedingly intelligent paranoiac'. 'You believe in the God who plays dice', Einstein wrote to Max Born in 1944, 'and I in complete law and order in a world which objectively exists . . .' But experiments have supported the dice-playing view of small matter.

Einstein's own theories of relativity, meanwhile, further

subverted Newton's clockwork universe. Einstein provided a new way of understanding space, mass and energy. The special theory of relativity, laid out by Einstein in 1905, contradicts our intuitive view of time and space. They were not, he said, fixed or absolute quantities. They were subjective: where an observer stood determined his view of what happened when and where. In 1916, Einstein's general theory of relativity explained gravitation as the warping of space and time by physical mass; space itself was curved. Time was not independent of space. Time acted like a fourth dimension of space, and time too could be warped by gravity. Events took place not in time, but in a 'space–time continuum'. Space and time might not be realities of nature at all, but rather simple psychological effects. Because the shape of space–time depended on gravity, space and time would make no sense if humans didn't have bodies. 'It was formerly believed', he said, 'that if all material things disappeared out of the universe, time and space would be left. According to the relativity theory, however, time and space disappear together with the things.'

Despite the weirdness of relativity and quantum mechanics, they had dramatic practical effects, including nuclear bombs, nuclear power, transistors, computers and modern cosmology.

How the West fell out of love with science

Up to 1900, the progress of science excited hopes that the earlier simplicity of religious world-views would be replaced by a more accurate but equally simple scientific explanation, making it easier and easier to understand the world. But ever since, it seems, science has made understanding reality more difficult. As Jean-François Lyotard said, modern science 'is producing not the known but the unknown'.[21] It is not surprising that this version of science has less

---

21 Jean-François Lyotard (1984) *The Post-Modern Condition: A Report on Knowledge*, Manchester University Press, Manchester.

popular appeal. Imagine that in 1687 Newton had discovered relativity theory rather than his laws of motion and gravity. Would we ever have had the confidence to invent the steam engine, modern agriculture, cheap textiles, railways, electricity, steel, automobiles or airplanes, or believe that we could improve society by political and social action? Would magic and superstition have yielded to reason?

Insofar as it *is* possible for the layperson to catch the drift of modern science, the message is unwelcome. Up to the mid-nineteenth century, science seemed compatible with a benevolent divine order and with our special role as co-agent with God in creating a better world. The view presented by Darwin's theories in 1859 and by the discoveries of twentieth-century science appeared much less hospitable to God and humans.

It used to be thought that science would bestow huge benefits on the world, and science used to be able to meet these expectations. Trust in science perhaps reached its zenith with the moon landings and safe return of the Apollo astronauts in 1969. But already there was a strong counter-current in the public appreciation of science, which had begun in the inter-war years with the perception, evident for example in Aldous Huxley's *Brave New World* (1932), that science was de-humanizing, too easily the tool of dictators and privileged elites. Suspicion of science was hugely multiplied and deepened by the horrors of Hiroshima, and the very real fear, given ample justification in the 1962 Cuban missile crisis, that nuclear arsenals could wipe out human civilization. Eminent scientists voiced their doubts. 'If I had known they were going to do this,' said Einstein after Hiroshima, 'I would have become a shoemaker.' Bertrand Russell, the distinguished British philosopher and mathematician, led huge 'Ban the Bomb' protest marches in the 1950s and 1960s. After 1969, the more muted exploration of space never fully recaptured the public imagination.

From the 1960s, evidence began to pile up that science's triumphs had already begun to poison the planet's water, air and soil. The greenhouse effect, the depletion of the ozone layer and the subversion of earth's ecosystem; the destruction of the Amazonian rain forest; and the alarming proliferation and increased availability of nuclear, chemical and biological weapons were all seen as the fruits of science. Astronomer Martin Rees estimates that humanity only has a 50–50 chance of surviving the next century without a major catastrophe threatening life itself.[22]

In the late nineteenth century, and for most of the twentieth, faith in religion declined and faith in science grew. In the later twentieth century, as faith in science faltered, faith in religion revived; equally, as faith in religion rose, faith in science fell still further. After 1990, some 35 to 40 per cent of Americans, and a smaller but still significant proportion of other Westerners, identified themselves as 'born again' Christians. They believe that the Bible is the infallible Word of God, and that the creation of the world was accurately described by the account in Genesis.

The Creationist dogma is, perhaps, more unscientific than anti-scientific. More worrying for science and faith in reason is evidence of a popular Western, and especially American, descent to superstition, going beyond the fundamentalist minority. A 1999 poll showed that 77 per cent of Americans believed in 'angels, that is, some kind of heavenly beings who visit earth' and 73 per cent believe that angels 'come into the world in these modern days'. Polls also show that a quarter of Americans believe in astrological predictions (and another 22 per cent are not sure), that almost half believe that people can be possessed by demons, 57 per cent believe in telepathy or other forms of extra-sensory perception, and 60 per cent believe in the existence of Satan. A *Newsweek* poll in 1996 said that 48 per cent of Americans believed in UFOs and that 27 per cent believed that aliens had visited the earth. In 1997, CNN reported that 50 per cent of

---

22 Martin Rees (2004) *Our Final Century? Will the Human Race Survive the Twenty-First Century?* Arrow, London.

Americans believed that aliens have abducted humans, that 64 per cent believed that aliens had visited earth, and that 80 per cent thought that their government was hiding knowledge of the existence of aliens.

The polls indicate a revival of belief in magic that has no precedent since the Middle Ages. It is difficult to know how seriously to take what people tell pollsters. Certainly, respondents claiming allegiance to a pre-scientific world-view or to the occult invariably connect to the Internet through scientific means and prefer airlines to flying broomsticks. Strange beliefs do not preclude rational behaviour.

What is clear, however, is the growth in the last half-century of anti-intellectualism. Influenced by television and by the fashionable doctrines of relativism – that one view is as good as another – we are witnessing the elevation of emotion over reason, of personal 'relevance' and conviction over hard thinking.

Does loss of faith in science matter?

Science seems impervious to the attacks upon it. To a greater degree than ever, the world is being shaped by science. Whether through ever more sophisticated weaponry, the development of new technologies such as cellular phones, the personal computer and the Internet, the expansion of new therapies and medical procedures, or the proliferation of research and education, science is on the march and penetrating every corner of the globe and of our daily lives. Scientific advance is unstoppable, constant and cumulative. There is no substitute for Western science, no other way of combining observation and theory, of harnessing the world to human purposes, of making things work better. There is no 'alternative' science, no Buddhist science, no New Age science, no relativist science, no fundamentalist science. The West retains its scientific dominance. In the 1990s, the United States won 44 Nobel Prizes, Germany five, France three, and Japan, despite spending fully half the US level on scientific funding, just one.[23]

It is science that defines the wealth and power of nations and individuals. Compared to science, the influence of social classes, occupational groups, political leaders, political parties, social movements, or any other engine of history, all fade into the background. Only the equally remorseless spread of our new post-capitalist economic system – outlined in the next chapter – constitutes a parallel and complementary force of comparable importance in determining the future of the world; and the new economic system is substantially derived from science itself.

It might, therefore, appear that science can slough off its lower popular standing. The funds for science keep coming, as does a ready supply of highly educated scientists. But pause. Reflect on the intellectual causes of modern science: belief in God and belief in humanity, a rational world-view and optimism about humanity's place in the cosmos. Science appears to have disposed of belief in the causes of science. Science has eaten away at its thought-foundations. If this is true and irrevocable, what is left? 'Only' technology, the search for profit and humanity's ineradicable intellectual curiosity. We put 'Only' in quotation marks because technology, business and imagination are fantastic motivators and enablers. Science will continue to thrive. But the contribution of science to human meaning, the human spirit, and the non-material richness of civilization have shrivelled. Knowledge itself, instead of exciting and uniting Westerners at large, is in danger of becoming a minority taste, corralled into universities, research institutes and corporations, barricaded against the new breed of

---

23 Explanations for the slight accomplishments of Eastern science generally focus on three factors: a tendency to support mediocre older scientists rather than brilliant young ones; the absence of debate and confrontation; and perhaps, most importantly, Eastern patterns of thought, which respect complexity and hesitate to formulate simple hypotheses of cause and effect. As Richard Nisbett says, 'In science . . . you get closer to the truth more quickly by riding roughshod over complexity.'

barbarians, those already within the city gates, flaunting their ignorance and wallowing in the warm bath of emotional imbecility. Some of the new barbarians were 'educated' in our universities; they are articulate, intelligent and cynical in promoting anti-intellectual values. They are leading the less gifted, not toward knowledge and civilization, but toward their negation.

Of course, we exaggerate. There are still idealistic scientists, there are still educated and knowledge-loving citizens, and science still retains some moral authority. But the ideal of a society based on reason and knowledge is receding.

Three ways forward

First, let's be clear that meaning is *not* destroyed by science. Science operates on a technical level, removed from moral and religious judgements. Science is not opposed to religion; even in modern times, a majority of American scientists describe themselves as religious.[24] Science is complemented by other forms of knowledge, by philosophy or religion, which address the human quest for meaning.

Second, the new scientific paradigm – the image of a random, arbitrary universe – may well be a dangerous, inaccurate and unnecessary simplification. The micro-world acts in a weird way, yet scientists have not abandoned the scientific method, and for good reason. The vast majority of science is susceptible to reason,

---

24 In the latest available detailed and large-scale survey, that of the Carnegie Commission of 1969, based on a sample of 60,028 American Academics, 55 per cent of scientists in the physical and life sciences describe themselves as religious, as do 60 per cent of mathematicians and statisticians. Only 27 per cent of the latter, 27 per cent of physical scientists, and 29 per cent of life scientists said they had no religion. It is interesting that the proportion of social scientists who were religious was significantly lower, at 45 per cent, with psychologists (33 per cent) and anthropologists (29 per cent) the least religious. We suspect that the opposition between religion and science has been exaggerated by social scientists who may subconsciously have been extrapolating from their own views and those of their colleagues.

experimentation, verification and falsification. We cannot yet understand the smallest forms of matter in fully rational terms, but that does not imply an irrational universe.

Scientists are prone to reduce the complexity of their findings to 'thought-bites' which are unconsciously influenced more by society's latest fashionable ideas than by the inherent truth of their research. Darwin is an excellent example. Darwin himself, and Herbert Spencer, whom Darwin immensely admired and praised, believed that Darwin's insight into the origin of species naturally implied the superiority of the European races over all others. As everyone now acknowledges, this was toxic nonsense. There is nothing in *On the Origin of Species* which justifies, or even attempts to justify, the racist 'implications' almost universally drawn by the subsequent generation of biologists. No Darwinian now believes them. Yet Darwin was a brilliant scientist, a decent, honest and gentle man! His theory resonated with a pre-formed view of European racial ascendancy, giving it renewed and fateful impetus.

Will scientists in 50 or 100 years – if there are any – still admire quantum physics, but shake their heads with wonder at the idea that it proved that the universe was irrational?

Third, *even if* – which is unproven, and, we think, unlikely – current and future scientific discoveries do lead conclusively to the most pessimistic conclusions about life and the universe, to the explanation that there is no meaning in them, that civilization is just an accident, or even an illusion; then does this mean there is no hope?

We do not think so. What we may call the 'lonely hypothesis' – that there is no rational and good God, and probably no God at all, that humankind is a speck of insignificance on the edge of a vast, pointless universe, doomed to return sooner or later to the nothingness from which we came – has its own splendour, inspiration and self-justification. If there is no meaning in the universe, how glorious of humanity to have created so much from so little! The achievements of our own civilization are enough to justify the universe, even if the justification is heard in utter silence or indifference by whatever non-human force or forces there may or may not be. If nothing else will supply meaning in the universe, the existence and achievements of human intellect, creativity and love are quite enough.

Conclusion

We draw four conclusions. One: science is, in its fully developed form, a Western phenomenon. Two: at the root of science lies the stimulus of two other great Western ideas – the Christian belief in a perfect, powerful and rational Creator; and optimism about the nature of humanity. Three: science has suffered because twentieth-century science, and, more importantly, new fashionable fancies, have undermined belief in precisely these two great ideas. Four: there is far too little justification to abandon our trust in rationality and in science, for the best forms of civilization depend utterly upon them.

5 Growth

About 200 years ago, rather suddenly in historical terms, economic growth in the West became unstoppable. The history of mankind up to that point had been one of modest or zero growth. Population and living standards were flattened by nature, above all by hunger and disease. Between 1750 and 1820, England entered the machine age. Machines brought automatic growth, a novel phenomenon. With the steam engine and industry, growth spread rapidly throughout the West. Within a century, economic growth had brought world domination to the West.

The arrival of self-extending growth is arguably the most important change in human history, making humanity a biological success, able to live long and safe lives and multiply numbers and living standards enormously. Industrial growth also upended society, divided it into new classes, concentrated it in cities, created vast hierarchies, desecrated the countryside, raped the planet, drained the spirit of humanity, and helped to lead to unprecedented centralization of power. Industrialization also led to experimentation with, and conflict between, two new economic systems – capitalism and 'statism' (control by the communist or Nazi state).

As we know, capitalism won – but only just, only after enormously destructive convulsions. Capitalism proved, eventually, a much better economic system; but for more than 100 years it appeared, to the great majority of intellectuals, and to the bottom half of the population, to be deeply unattractive. All this, too, was the legacy of automatic growth. In 1900 the West was triumphant and seemed united in its civilization. In 1914, nationalism shattered the peace. From 1917 to 1989, Russian communism set about building a new world, whose model came from the West but was implacably hostile to the whole Western world.

Today, economic growth rolls on. Capitalism has been domesticated, broadly accepted, and extended well beyond the West. But something new is happening. In the West, a superior economic system is gradually supplanting capitalism. The new system – which we call the 'personalized economy'– provides equal or greater sustainable growth, with far less use of capital, less plunder of the planet, and less human alienation. But the personalized economy has one huge drawback. Or two, if you count the fact that it will be very difficult for non-Western countries to adopt it.

How the West acquired automatic growth

In 1750, the West was not much more prosperous than the Rest. Before 1400, China had come within a hair's breadth of industrializing. Though industrialization was aborted by regime change and an introverted economy, between 1500 and 1820 China consistently accounted for between a third and a fifth of total world output. Before 1750, the most advanced European countries only had a *per capita* income between one-and-a-half and twice that of China, compared to America's current lead over China of more than nine times.[1]

With the automatic growth implanted by industrialization, the West started to pull ahead. Even by 1820, out of 24 countries for which we have estimates of income per head, Western countries took the top 15 places, followed by Mexico, Finland, Russia, and then five non-Western countries, with China's income per head

---

1 Measured in terms of purchasing power, the fairer measure, China currently has a *per capita* income of just over $3,500, compared to the US at just over $32,000. Measured at actual market exchange rates, the figures are $856 and $36,154 respectively, a US superiority of 42 times. See Roger Bootle (2005) *Money for Nothing: Real Wealth, Financial Fantasies, and the Economy of the Future*, Nicholas Brealey, London, pp. 146–7.

only 30 per cent of the level of the UK (figures are adjusted to take out the effect of inflation, and are expressed in modern values, or to be more precise, 1990 dollar equivalents; see Table 5.1).[2]

Table 5.1: Income per head in 1820 ($ equivalents)

UK	1,756	Norway	1,004
Netherlands	1,561	Ireland	954
Australia	1,528	Canada	893
Austria	1,295	Czechoslovakia	849
Belgium	1,291	Mexico	760
USA	1,287	Finland	759
Denmark	1,225	Russia	751
France	1,218	Japan	704
Sweden	1,198	Brazil	670
Germany	1,112	Indonesia	614
Italy	1,092	India	531
Spain	1,063	China	523

It wasn't entirely an accident that automatic growth arose first in the West. From about 900, agricultural productivity rose sharply following the invention of the stirrup, the mould-board plough, and the horse collar. European city-states gradually flourished and became increasingly autonomous, as free craftsmen, traders and other burghers comprised a growing middle layer of society, neither lord nor peasant. Over the following centuries, European inventors became astonishingly prolific. A small sample of inventions shows the range and influence: the blast furnace, canal lock, chimney, coal fire, glass window, marine chart, water wheel, printing press, spectacles, suction pump, treadle loom, water-driven bellows, weight-driven clock and windmill. The first ever patent – for a canal boat rigged with cranes – was granted in Florence in 1421.

2   John Kay (2003) *The Truth About Markets*, Penguin, London, quoting the most recent study available (undertaken in 1992 and covering the period 1820–1990).

There is a clear link between individual creativity and a degree of political freedom; between trade and technology on the one hand, and the increased autonomy of artisans and merchants in their city-states. As one economic historian writes:

At the root of technological progress is . . . [an] environment that makes it possible for inventors to be heard . . . [suggesting] that free speech and an openness to persuasion leads to riches. When the Europeans, or at least some of them, stopped torturing, beheading and burning each other, the economy grew. No wonder that the nations where speech was free by contemporary standards were the first to grow rich: Holland, Scotland, England, Belgium and the United States.[3]

Out went the aristocratic ideal of military glory and bloodthirsty plunder. In came the merchant ideal of 'gentle commerce' – where hard work can take an artisan to modest prosperity, and different territories trade peacefully. In the eighteenth century, Voltaire said that commerce facilitated liberty and united humankind: '. . . the Jew, the Mahometan, and the Christian transact together as tho' they all profess'd the same religion . . . as trade enriched the citizens in England, so it contributed to their freedom, and this freedom on the other side extended their Commerce'.[4]

This was an urban ideology – it grew with cities. In 1500 there were only five European cities with 100,000 inhabitants; by 1600 there were 14.[5] England grew fastest – from sustaining a population of 4.1 million in 1600, sharp improvements in agricultural productivity, and the early stirrings of workshop industry, raised the

3 I. Kirtzner (1989) *Discovery, Capitalism and Distributive Justice*, Blackwell, Oxford.

4 Voltaire (1994) *Letters Concerning the English Nation*, Oxford University Press, New York, p. 30.

5 Amsterdam, Antwerp, Constantinople, Lisbon, Marseilles, Messina, Milan, Moscow, Naples, Palermo, Paris, Rome, Seville and Venice. Half were important ports; all were trading centres.

population to 5.7 million by 1750. Then came takeoff. In 1771, Richard Arkwright, a barber and wig-maker turned inventor, opened the world's first large-scale spinning mill on the banks of the River Derwent, five floors high, each of 3,000 square feet, powered by waterwheel and using Arkwright's own patented water frame for cotton spinning. In 1776 the Scottish middle-class 'mechanic', James Watt, made the first commercially viable steam engine. By 1787 Britain boasted 145 cotton mills. The factory system was born.

Machines took on a life of their own. Previously, output was chained to horsepower and human physical effort. Now machines could continually raise production levels and quality while steadily cutting product cost. The same number of people, leveraged by machines and money, could make more and more. The expansion of wealth created new markets and new employment. Although conditions were harsh, the English population tripled between 1750 and 1850, reaching 16.5 million – a population explosion never before seen without mass migration.

The real miracle was that growth became self-propelling – economic advance was limited only by the size of available markets, which kept growing as prosperity increased. If there was demand, industry could supply, and by applying technology and capital, constantly make goods better and cheaper. As Karl Marx noted, the machine system implied permanent revolution: 'Modern industry never looks upon . . . the existing form of process as final. The technical basis of that industry is therefore revolutionary, while all earlier modes of production were essentially conservative.'[6] The effect is growth in output per man-hour of about 3 per cent each year, which has been achieved, approximately, in every industrializing country of the world and throughout industrial history. Three per cent a year sounds modest, but it doubles living standards every 23 years.[7]

---

6 Karl Marx (1995) *Capital*, edited by David McLellan, Oxford University Press, Oxford, volume 1, chapter 15, section 9, pp. 291–2.

7 Some of the gain is reflected in shorter working hours, so incomes may not rise by three per cent a year, but over the long haul real hourly earnings do rise, reliably, by 3 per cent a year.

Growing pains

For 900 years before the machine age, Western society became steadily more autonomous and increasingly free. Europe, and later America, made progress through the expansion and energies of the rising urban middle classes, raising society's wealth and also advancing personal and political freedom. This 900-year upward curve of greater autonomy was rudely smashed by industrial capitalism. Wealth and growth proliferated as never before. But personal autonomy was curbed.

Whereas an independent agricultural worker or artisan could own his own tools, no individual worker could own and operate a steam engine. The worker became dwarfed by industry. As Marx said, 'It is no longer the laborer that employs the means of production, but the means of production that employ the laborer'[8] . . . 'Thus capital uses the worker, the worker does not use capital.'[9] Creative individuals such as Arkwright and Watt devised the technology of industry, but the machine-based economy grew increasingly centralized and capital-hungry. Ever greater and greater division of labour eclipsed individual discretion and creativity.

Enterprise became depersonalized. Whereas a single entrepreneur, family or group of individuals could own a plantation, a fleet of ships or a textile mill, the capital needs of railways, steel plants and the whole raft of mass manufacturing that evolved from the mid-nineteenth century, soon outpaced the cash and managerial skill of most families. The minimum capital level needed to compete effectively kept rising – there seemed no upper limit to effective scale.

Andrew Carnegie kept doubling the size of steel mills, concentrating more and more production into a single corporation; the cost of production kept falling and falling. The application of mass production to automobiles created a new capital-intensive industry

---

8   Karl Marx (1995), volume 1, chapter 11, p. 187.
9   Karl Marx, 'Results of the Immediate Process of Production', in *Capital*, p. 394.

that changed the face of America and concentrated market share to an extraordinary extent – whereas in the 1890s 500 carmakers fought for fragments of a the tiny American market, by 1965 three firms controlled 94 per cent of a massively greater market.

All the time, the number of workers, and capital, employed in corporations, their elaborate hierarchy, their central control of strategy, and their capital, grew and grew; the importance of the individual worker shrank and shrank. Only by organizing into larger and larger unions could workers exercise some countervailing power; but this was to fight centralization with centralization. The earnings of workers increased; their autonomy contracted.

The enormous hostility to capitalism from the mid-nineteenth to the mid-twentieth centuries has to be seen against this background. Communism, fascism and Nazism were dangerous because they tapped into a rich vein of anti-urban, anti-industrial, anti-materialist, anti-capitalist and anti-Semitic ideas, which, for all their irrationality and often murderous hate, rested on more than a grain of truth – that capitalism was spiritually enervating, destructive of the human spirit. It is this truth, originally propounded by early nineteenth-century European Romantics who hated the ugly, community-wrenching aspects of early industrialization, which still sustains the anti-growth and anti-capitalist movements.[10]

Today, the most persuasive anti-growth campaigners link anti-materialism to green values. They argue persuasively that, beyond a certain level of income, increased prosperity does not generate increased happiness . . . so what is the point of extra growth, growth that is unsustainable, eventually, given the finite limits of our planet's resources and the vast expansion of human numbers

---

10 Of course, communism in practice had all the same industrial defects as capitalism, only more so. 'State capitalism', as Trotsky rightly called the Soviet system, was even less individualistic and more alienating, and demanded more self-denial from workers in order to accumulate capital faster. In the USSR capital-building took nearly half of national income, whereas in the West it never exceeded a quarter.

and expectations? As noted by Milton and Rose Friedman: 'All the movements of the past two decades – the consumer movement, the ecology movement, the back-to-the-land movement, the protect-the-wilderness movement, the zero-population-growth movement, the "small is beautiful" movement, the anti-nuclear movement – have had one thing in common. All have been anti-growth.'[11] This 'green' critique finds intellectual and popular resonance. Yet electorates continue to demand growth.

The upshot is collective schizophrenia – we know growth is unsustainable, yet we can't kick the habit. Is there another approach, fully consistent with Western values and needs – to grow in ways that minimize the use of finite resources?

There may be a solution, at least for the West – we will come to that shortly. It may be worth pausing, however, to reflect that while the neglect of human spirituality may be terrible and self-defeating, there may also be much to be said in praise of material-ism. Anyone who has lived in a Third World country, or even a depressed spot in the West, can appreciate a little of the cost of poverty in terms of misery and affront to human dignity. It is not just the hunger, the cold, the sickness, the boredom, or the lack of hope for a better future. It is also the grinding down of feelings of self-worth, the inability to be optimistic and generous to friends and family, and the utter misery that makes it impossible to take joy in nature's finest features. A beautiful sunset may look less beautiful from skid row.

Even after modest affluence, materialism can actually lift and enhance the human spirit. Desiring a better future for one's children is a generous impulse, giving millions a useful purpose in life. Even the self-centred ambition to get on, to create a better life for oneself, inevitably gives a degree of constructive dynamism to society – in a market economy it will tend, if the go-getter is suc-cessful, to be because he or she has done something other people want. A degree of activism and forward motivation is what drives

---

11 Milton and Rose Friedman (1980) *Free to Choose*, Harcourt Brace, New York.

society toward improvement. Humans are, to greater or lesser degrees, self-aggrandizing animals. If ambition cannot be expressed constructively in the search for improved material conditions of life, it will be expressed in less constructive ways, such as the desire for power over people, or the imposition of cruelty in the service of a higher ideal. The mentality of the merchant, the manufacturer, the entrepreneur, the service provider, is materialistic. The mentality of the hero, the general and the state official – whether bureaucrat, churchman, or intellectual – will tend to be less materialistic. At times this may be fortunate; but it may often have less happy consequences. The materialism of the merchant is more *likely* to lead to peace and human welfare as well as prosperity. War is humankind's greatest temptation and scourge.

The issue with growth is not whether it is desirable – of course it is. Without growth, improvement of society and individuals is impossible; without growth, the human spirit wilts or is driven to destructive ends. Without growth, we cannot serve ourselves or society. Without growth, there is, by and large, no new music, no new architecture, no new painting, no new literature, no new science, no more convenient technology – not only no comfort, but also no civilization.

The issue is *what kind* of growth is desirable and possible. There is a hierarchy of human needs, as explained in 1970 by the industrial psychologist, Abraham Maslow;[12] and it applies to societies as well as to individuals. If a country is poor, it needs industrial growth. If a community is rich, it needs goods and services that use as few finite resources as possible and yet make life more enjoyable, more exciting, more social and more liberated. The greatest need, when all others have been satisfied, Maslow termed 'self-actualization'. This means the ability to enjoy work, to see it as an assertion of one's personality and development, and to choose how far to work and how far to pursue other means of creative self-expression.

---

12 Abraham H. Maslow (1970) *Motivation and Personality*, Harper & Row, New York.

The West's new economic system

As they become richer, industrial economies evolve. The early stages, focused on heavy industry and producer goods, pave the way for a more complex economy where consumer goods and personal services predominate. In the US and Britain this shift became significant in the 1950s. By 2000, it was irreversibly established throughout the West.

As consumers become affluent, they demand something a little better, different or customized. Brands cater to distinctive customer identities. Where new products used to be offered once a decade, they are now introduced every year or month. Choice trumps efficiency.

Technology responds to demand. Innovation used to make goods bigger and cheaper, through capital-intensive centralization. Now technology makes products modular, lighter, smaller, more flexible, more appealing, more personalized and usually cheaper too.

In the process, the economy is transformed. Value used to lie in raw materials and manufacturing – in natural resources and mass production factories, in returns to capital and blue-collar workers. Value now resides in design, marketing, software, delivery, customization. These activities are not mechanical, machine-driven, labour intensive or capital intensive. They are creative and personalized.

Even traditional manufacturing sectors – furniture, clothes, footwear – can be transformed. Across much of the world, mass production and cheap labour may continue to deliver most of what we wear and sit on; yet in the 1980s Italian entrepreneurs discovered a different way. Through innovative design, creativity and high quality, Italian producers, often family based, have thrived while traditional manufacturers in other rich countries, such as America and Britain, have all but disappeared.

Machines, and machine-like hierarchies within large organizations, can deliver efficiency. They cannot deliver fertile, ceaseless innovation. Well-oiled machines do not innovate spontaneously. Variation and fresh thinking are human attributes requiring education, independence and a dash of rebellion. Enthusiasm for the product becomes essential; the best innovations come from individuals who are ardent consumers of the 'new new thing'. Innovators query sacred cows. Innovators like a blank canvas; they like their own show.

Moving from efficiency to innovation creates a vast array of new markets, new products and new stages of production, where new companies led by people with new ideas can enter and grow at the expense of established, large, broad-line, integrated, capital-intensive firms. The innovators require relatively little capital; they avoid low-return, capital-intensive activities such as manufacturing. They sub-contract that to existing firms, who are suffering from huge overcapacity constantly thrown up by the relentless march of efficiency.

Even large capital-intensive firms must turn themselves inside out. Efficiency required centralization. Coping with change, choice, uppity customers and new competitors requires decentralization. Managers used to be loyal subordinates carrying out orders from on high. Now they have to become innovators, experimenters and risk-takers. This has one massively important, but little noticed, effect. There is a colossal transfer of actual or potential power from the corporation – its hierarchy and shareholders – to the individual.

Going beyond industry necessarily also means going beyond capitalism. Capitalism revolves around the need for capital accumulation – the scarce, most potent and decisive factor of production is capital. Employees play bit parts in an undifferentiated mass of workers. Profits gravitate to the owners of capital. Capitalism builds up ever larger, more capital-intensive, more profitable corporations, where power rests with the owners of capital because capital is productive and in short supply. Capitalism thrives on industrialism, centralization, regimentation, standardization, economies of scale, and being the largest and lowest cost producer.

It is a controlled system, stable, predictable and durable. Those who are interested in making money become captains of industry, but rarely significant owners of capital themselves.

In the West, this set-up is going; it is dwindling fast. The largest and most capital-intensive firms are declining in importance. The largest 100 US companies accounted for 62 per cent of stock market value in 1980, but only 46 per cent 20 years later. This understates the extent of the change, since many new and ultra-successful firms – Microsoft is the best example – are not capital intensive. Though Microsoft looks like a capitalist corporation, the greatest returns have been to its founders and employees, not to the providers of capital, who were and are totally unimportant. The whole mushrooming technology sector has very low capital intensity – ideas matter, not capital.

People who want to make money these days don't make their careers within established large industrial corporations. They become investment bankers, management consultants, head-hunters, brokers, venture capitalists, sports stars, rock stars, movie stars, bestselling authors, or entrepreneurs. In 1982 there were just 13 American billionaires. Now there are over 200. Even after taking account of inflation, more Americans have become billion-aires in the past 15 years than in all previous history.

The foremost force driving post-industrial creation is not land, nor labour, nor capital. It is human innovation – the human mind and human action. During the Industrial Revolution, inventors without capital were supplicants. A little innovation required piles of capital.

Today, bright people with the right idea can create millions or billions with little capital. In the late 1970s, two semi-hippies, Steve Jobs and Steve Wozniak, founded Apple, with the ambition of developing the first viable personal computer. They needed some capital, but not much, and they readily obtained it. First one sold his HP calculator, the other his Volkswagen, and then a friend, Intel executive Mike Markkula, became their partner, advancing $91,000. The Apple personal computer was born; the company became worth billions. Wozniak, disillusioned with corporate life, left Apple to spend his fortune bankrolling a series of rock groups before founding another company to innovate anew.

The *location of creation* has switched. Under industrial capitalism, *machines operating centrally* created riches. Arkwright and Kay invented the mechanized spinning frame, Watt perfected his steam engine, but then the machines took on a life of their own – the machines themselves churned out money. People danced around the edges, enlarging and improving the machines, putting them together in large mills or mines to turbo-boost productivity, adapting their pace of work to that of the machines. It was the *machines* that were so awesomely productive. The machines were in control.

Now it is not machines or their owners, but creative individuals who are centre-stage. People not only invent new technology; they *are* the new technology. In the personalized economy, the 'creative' industries – ranging from architecture, publishing, design and software, to music, broadcasting, entertainment, sport and the arts – are growing at double the rate of the economy as a whole and four times faster than the old industries of production and distribution. The creative industries' raw material is ecological – people and ideas. Machines leverage, but do not usurp, the human imagination. As sociologist Manuel Castells says:

> For the first time in history, the human mind is a direct productive force, not just a decisive element of the production system. Thus, computers, communication systems, and genetic decoding and programming are all amplifiers and extensions of the human mind.[13]

It's difficult to envisage a more total switch from centralization to decentralization, from machines to men and women, from disem-

---

13 Manuel Castells (1996) *The Rise of the Network Society,* Blackwell Publishers, Malden, MA.

bodied impersonal power to personalized power, from the confined past to the boundless possibilities of tomorrow . . . and from capital to individuals.

In the West, *knowledge has become personalized.* Though much valuable knowledge remains with government and corporations, the new trend is for really valuable knowledge to become the property of individuals.

In 1947, William Shockley invented the transistor. Shockley was employed by Bell Labs, owned by AT&T. By a quirk of US regulation, AT&T, which enjoyed a near monopoly of the telephone network, was unable to exploit Shockley's discovery. Shockley set up Fairchild Semiconductor; Fairchild, in turn, spawned a remarkable number of Silicon Valley spin-offs. Thousands of Silicon Valley engineer-entrepreneurs have since made fortunes out of ideas they have adapted from the intellectual gene pool of the Valley, ideas that rested originally on more fundamental ideas from Stanford University, government research programmes and corporate research and development. Very largely, taxpayers and shareholders paid for the knowledge; individuals reaped the reward. Yet it is very doubtful that the explosion of new ideas and breakthrough products in California would have been anywhere near as great without allowing individuals to leverage old ideas to develop new ones, and to benefit personally. This is how open and dynamic societies work.

Professor Henry Chesbrough of Harvard Business School says that before 1980 'closed innovation' prevailed – research was conducted secretly, within large corporations.[14] Thereafter, products were increasingly developed through 'open innovation' – ideas flowed from many different sources, with active participation by universities, high mobility of labour and therefore of ideas, an enthusiastic venture capital market, and many highly productive start-ups.

---

14 Henry Chesbrough (2003) *Open Innovation: The New Imperative for Creating and Profiting from Technology,* Harvard Business School Press, Boston.

Industrial giants such as IBM moved to open innovation because they had to. IBM used to take the top students in physics, mathematics and computer science. After 1950, however, university computer science departments proliferated on a wave of government funding. The best graduates now had a choice. They could wear white shirts at IBM, or wear what they liked on campus. As faculty members, they could purchase and tinker with fresh technologies and products from venture capital-backed firms such as DEC. IBM once had a monopoly of ideas and computer science talent almost as strong as its monopoly of computers themselves. By losing the former, IBM forfeited the latter.

The effect of open innovation is to transfer initiative and wealth from established corporations to new ones, and from shareholders to individuals.

One more vignette: biotechnology. For four decades, the US National Science Foundation and the National Institutes of Health poured over $100 billion, in today's money, into biotech research, training thousands of post-graduate biotechnologists. Nobody knew whether there would ever be a commercial payoff. When it arrived, from the 1990s, biotechnologists rushed to start their own firms. The massive biotech research funding is now being recycled into stock market value: as we write, two companies alone, Amgen and Genentech, have a combined value of $129 billion. Clearly, the total biotech industry will recover much more than $100 billion. Where are these billions going? Not back to government, and very little to old-style pharmaceutical titans, whose biotech research has consistently disappointed. The bonanza is going to individual executives and their venture capital backers.

Not only knowledge, but also competition, has become personalized. Individual executives can exert a major influence on the strategic position of their firm, by joining a competitor, or by becoming one. If capital is needed to start a business, venture capitalists – who themselves are professionals who start with no capital and take a large slice personally – will fund good ideas and good people.

From thought to action, individuals are at the heart of creation, innovation and wealth creation. Every element of unique human personality takes part in creation – intellect, imagination, emotion, calculation, empathy, communication, action and reaction. So, far from being impersonal, every important business action has become personalized, verging on the artistic.[15]

You don't need to start a corporation to escape from the power of capital. You can become a one-person business, or join a small group of partners, and do tomorrow precisely what you do today – but on your own account. Plumbers and accountants, cab drivers and movie stars, estate agents and professional sportspeople, cleaners and rock stars, personal trainers and architects . . . the list of self-employed people, often refugees from the capitalist sector, is very long. If individuals own the means of productions – their own brains, their arms and legs, their computers, their screwdrivers, their cars – then they need not work under capitalism. Self-employed workers are not in the capitalist sector. Even workers in capitalist corporations are now sometimes treated as individuals – rewarded, more and more, on the basis of individual contribution, not as part of a mass of workers. When work has become individualized, the employment contract must become individualized too; even the stick-in-the-mud employee, if highly skilled, has a chance of taking surplus value from shareholders.

In all kinds of ways, therefore, we are moving away from capitalism, from an economy centred on capital and large, established, hierarchical corporations.[16] But we are not moving from private

---

15 It has been said that modern, liberal Western society is unique in according such a high place to the artist and artistic creation. If so, it is easy to understand why it is only in such a society that business could become so creative. Had they lasted a thousand years, could one imagine either the Third Reich or the Soviet Empire spawning the personal computer?

16 Of course, the personalized economy will not *completely* or immediately replace capitalism, just as capitalism did not completely or immediately replace the agricultural economy. What happens is that the new economy is layered upon the old one, which suffers first a relative decline and then an absolute one. The new driving force and growth today is a different, personalized economy, although capitalism will still be important in parts of the Western economy (and very important outside the West) for a long time to come.

hierarchy to public hierarchy, from capitalism to socialism or communism. We are moving towards a system that is even more market-oriented than capitalism, and much more decentralized. We are moving to a world where the individual, autonomous person is central – to the *personalized economy*.

What is different now is that value is driven by innovation, and innovation is driven by people. Capitalism and state socialism were powered by machines, testing the limits of human alienation. But people cannot be both alienated and inventive. The logic of capitalism is expansion and money making; but nowadays expansion and money making require dismantling all impediments to human creativity. That is why capitalism is allowing, even encouraging, human autonomy – but also why capitalism, piece by piece, is steadily dismantling itself.

The upshot is the reunification of social and personal progress with economic progress. In the 'long march of history', capitalism was an aberration, an anomaly. Whereas for 800 years, Europe, and later America, made progress through the expansion and energies of the rising urban middle classes, resulting in economic growth *and* the advance of personal and political freedom, industrial capitalism tore this unity apart. Capitalism brought enormous economic advances, but it also marginalized the individual producer and centralized the economy and society. The personalized economy reverts to the long-term Western trend of advancing wealth and freedom together. The progress of the personalized economy in the West is irreversible, except in the very unlikely event that the state imposes a new system by force. For those of us who fear the suicide of the West, economic developments are the most benign counter-indicator.

Except, that is, for the looming shadow of ecological suicide.

The prime problem with growth in population and the economy – perhaps the biggest issue of our century – is its run-down of finite resources (forests, fish stocks, soil, fossil fuels, plants, animal species, air, sunlight, water, space) and run-up in damage to the environment (toxic chemicals, atmospheric gases, non-indigenous

plant species). The automatic growth that came with the industrial–machine age spread during the twentieth century well beyond
the West. If countries outside the US, Europe and Japan eventually
reach current Western consumption levels, the negative effect on
resources and the environment would be multiplied *twelve times*.[17]
It is impossible for the earth to sustain such impact.

Toward a greener economy

The personalized economy offers a partial solution to this issue of
sustainability – by harnessing what is called 'weightlessness'.

Industrial economies are 'heavy' – value means weight. Virtually
all industrial progress from 1750 to 1950 involved building bigger
and bigger heavy industrial facilities. As economies grew, more and
more heavy products such as steel, cement, iron, tractors, cars,
tanks and aircraft were produced.

Since 1950, however, progress meant the proliferation of ever
lighter and *smaller* products and services. The first computers were
immensely heavy, the size of several football pitches. Greater
computing power now nestles in a laptop. Most of a computer's
value used to lie in its hardware; it's now in software. Is anything
else requiring so little space and energy as useful as a computer?
The World Wide Web, too, magically annihilates weight and
distance.

Of course, some products, like the automobile, still weigh a lot.
But even with cars, the new way to add value is to subtract weight
and add light features, usually through software upgrades. A third
of a new car's cost, and much more of its value, comes from
software.

In the move from capitalism to the personalized economy,
personal services of all kinds comprise a greater and greater share of
total output. Products are becoming lighter, but (though of course

---

17 Jared Diamond (2005).

we still need machines and objects) they are also becoming less important. Hence the economy can grow, yet not consume more resources. The value of United States output is estimated to have increased about twenty times since 1900, yet it weighs no more.[18]

Thus, perhaps, the green nightmare recedes. The personalized economy is not capital-intensive, nor materials-intensive, nor, to the same degree, energy-intensive. It is human-intensive. The human mind and spirit expands; industry and materials usage contract. It is now possible to imagine strong economic growth coexisting with significant decreases in the use of finite resources. The trend towards a greener economy is happening naturally, but it could be reinforced by government, private and individual initiatives.

The nightmare may recede, but it will not disappear. The West becomes greener, in part, by outsourcing its production to the rest of the world. There is less materials use and pollution in the Rust Belt of America, but there is more in Manila and cities throughout the industrializing world. Only if the personalized economy became global could it solve the green issue – and that is not going to happen in a hurry.

Two downsides to the personalized economy

One is galloping inequality. Capitalism is often blamed for inequality, but this is a misperception. Over time, under pressure from employees and society, capitalism's big corporations reached deals with the unions, and exerted an equalizing influence. Surveys have consistently shown that, until recently, unskilled and semi-skilled workers in large companies, provided they were unionized, were paid 30 to 40 per cent more than their counterparts in small business.

---

18 Diane Coyle (2001) *Paradoxes of Prosperity*, Texere, New York; and Diane Coyle (1997) *The Weightless World*, Capstone, Oxford.

Big business, however, can no longer be so munificent. Large firms are being squeezed on all sides – by more demanding shareholders, eager for higher profits; by the really valuable workers, whose loss to the corporation could be lethal; and by new, smaller, nimbler and meaner competitors, who prosper by rewarding the strong at the expense of the weak. Corporations are downsizing, cutting out layers, putting workers on casual contracts, hiring cheaper part-time and seasonal workers, and cutting pay for the unskilled. Individual results are being monitored much more closely. Passengers are being ejected. All this is not the fault of capitalism, or of managers, who much prefer paternalism, or the quiet life, to playing Scrooge. The blame rests squarely with the trend from capitalism toward the personalized economy. And, without destroying the many benefits brought by an economy based on individualism and creativity, society as a whole, through democratic decision-making, is the only means of protecting people marginalized in the process.

Talent is not equally distributed within the population, but it is not horribly skewed either. The problem is that the ability to make money is. Making millions is not a mark of virtue, as Calvinists and the rich may think. Making money is part luck, part opportunity, part stealing great ideas and adapting them, part hustle, and part sheer commercial genius. Whatever the mix, a very small percentage of the population will make a very large percentage of income. That is the problem with so-called meritocracy under decentralized and personalized markets.

The second drawback of the personalized economy is that it is increasing, and likely to continue increasing, the gap between the West and the Rest. One of the great things about capitalism was that it could fairly easily be transplanted to other economies. The machine-like nature of capitalism meant that with an economy open to the West, and investor-friendly policies, capitalism could be imported almost as a turnkey system. Large Western corporations could be enticed in or imitated, technology and working methods could be imported, and hey presto! An economic miracle! Importing capitalism was not very difficult.

The personalized economy is not like that. It requires liberal, even libertarian, political and social conditions. It requires a high degree of technological originality. It requires an educational system that, at least at its apex, encourages divergent thinking. It requires the rebellious spirit. It requires legal policies and attitudes that support the individual against the state and the private corporation. It requires that people do their own thing.

Capitalism is much more adaptable, even promiscuous. It burgeoned under aristocratic regimes, such as England from 1760 to 1867, and Imperial Japan, from the nineteenth century until 1945; under dictatorships such as those of Generals Franco, Salazar and Pinochet; in slave-owning America and democratic America; under post-war European and Japanese social democracy; in South East Asia since 1970, where fragile democracy has jostled with authoritarian and corrupt cliques; under South Africa's apartheid regime, and its democratic black government; and even, rather impressively, in repressive Red China.

Partly for reasons of government policy, and mainly for more fundamental reasons of history, outlook and inclination, it will be much more difficult for non-Western countries to mimic the personalized economy than it was for them to mimic capitalism. Creativity in business, as much as in science and the arts, requires intellectual conflict and the chaos of a libertarian society.

Conclusion

Automatic economic growth was a Western invention, leading to unprecedented growth in population, longevity and affluence. Industrial growth is spreading everywhere, bringing the same immediate benefits but causing massive and unsustainable damage to the planet. Meanwhile, the West has moved from industrial capitalism to the personalized economy, which is based on individual imagination. The personalized economy is a huge improvement on capitalism, greatly improving individual freedom for creative professionals and reducing the harm that growth does to the environment.

In spawning machine-based economies, the West may have led the world to the brink of ecological suicide. The only hope is the global replacement of industrial capitalism by the personalized economy. Currently this looks unlikely. To succeed in creating a personalized economy means adopting and embracing Western values. It means not just becoming like the West – it means becoming part of the West.

6   Liberalism

All Western societies are organized by liberal principles and institutions, in a way that very few non-Western societies are. That Western societies are liberal is a very lucky accident, and, as we will shortly show, deeply rooted in the peculiar history of the West. But first we need to define what we mean by liberal society.

A liberal society is one which is not only fully democratic, but where there is a spirit of freedom, fairness and respect for all citizens. Liberal civilization, compared to other civilizations, attaches greater importance to the sanctity and dignity of human life, to the education of all its people, to equality of opportunity, to the freedom of the individual and the full development of his or her talents, to the elimination of prejudice against individuals and groups, to the promotion of science and the arts, to the invention of better, cheaper and more convenient products, to the relief of suffering, and to the essential equality of brotherhood of all humankind. Liberal society is not institutionally corrupt or cruel; it is not ruled by the police or the military; it is not hierarchical or bureaucratic. Power in liberal societies is decentralized. There is freedom of the press and other media; freedom for business to operate, constrained only by requirements of honesty and humane standards; and tolerance of unconventional behaviour as long as it does not harm others. The government is subordinate to the rule of law. The state exists to serve citizens, and to increase their health, wealth, and to protect them from arbitrary force and oppression of any kind. Liberal societies do not believe in military glory; war is a last resort, primarily for self-protection. In practice, liberal states almost never declare war on other liberal states.

Liberal civilization never arrived fully fledged at a particular time, nor without a struggle for liberty. Every liberal society has emerged through a long process of adaptation, through the rise of individuals and groups determined to increase their freedom and autonomy, and through the forced or voluntary cessation of power by elites. The expansion of political liberty, and of institutions that restrain the powerful and treat all citizens fairly and equally, is only part of the process. Usually through the growth of economic power, individuals, occupational groups and classes gain self-respect and self-confidence, and the respect, grudging or otherwise, of the dominant elements of society. Liberty sometimes takes a leap forward as a result of political conflict, but liberty has never arrived in any society purely through force. Tolerance, mutual self-interest and the ability to cooperate and adapt to changed circumstances are characteristics by which liberal society both emerges and sustains itself.

Liberal democracy is the only way of organizing society that allows it to experiment fully, proceeding through trial and error, allowing government to change along with circumstances and without violence. Free and independent citizens, endowed with a degree of education, initiative and self-reliance, are not so much the result of a liberal society as a precondition for its advent. Yet liberal societies extend dignity to all citizens and take care of those who genuinely cannot take care of themselves. If the society is wealthy enough, it commits itself to abolish poverty.

Liberal societies are marked by freedom of religion and conscience, openness, widespread tolerance, the ability to collaborate, and the willingness of citizens to take responsibility for their actions. Liberal civilization can permit universal freedom without inducing anarchy because the law is impartial and respected, because the political process commands consent, and because citizens can trust each other to behave reasonably. In liberal societies, law does not defer to status; the political process ensures that the state serves the individual and not the other way round; and there is a sense of common membership of society. No fully liberal society has ever arisen without substantial ownership of property by ordinary citizens, or without a widespread sense of shared values and tacit commitment to the society and its institutions. Liberal societies are tolerant of new or unusual behaviour because there is a sense of common membership and identity uniting even the most disparate groups. Finally, the most liberal societies have always been a source of reference and inspiration for people struggling for freedom, and have always seen the value in identifying with other liberal societies, at least partly because of a common view of how to build an attractive and successful civilization. Liberal societies are able to take a critical view of their defects and imperfections, and to work toward closing the gap between reality and continually advancing liberal aspirations, while not losing sight of how far they have come or forfeiting a proper pride in the value of freedom.

The performance of liberal states is extraordinary. Despite many defects, they produce longer and healthier lives, more comfort and freedom, greater artistic energy, more distinguished and useful science, and less suffering than any other way of organizing society. Liberal societies enjoy higher living standards than non-liberal states. Without using terror or compulsion, liberal societies have created moral progress, steadily enlarging, as philosopher Peter Singer has shown,[1] the circle of those receiving our compassion – extending rights to all humanity, including children, women, slaves, foreigners, other races, the mentally ill, the handicapped, the dying, criminals and prisoners of war. Liberal society has stressed the importance of collective decisions and actions, reconciling individual freedom with group initiatives – most powerful when legitimated by the state, yet carried out spontaneously and voluntarily – for mutual support and the enrichment of life for the poor and oppressed. Liberal societies are always reaching out for further moral improvement, seeing the possibility of extending the

---

1   Peter Singer (1981) *The Expanding Circle: Ethics and Socio-biology*, Farrar, Straus & Giroux, New York.

circle of rights to take in animals, species, the environment and our planet's entire ecosystem.

Liberal civilization has demonstrated not only that freedom can coexist with greater prosperity, but also that freedom is a condition for the full development of individual talents and society's wealth. In economic terms, freedom is not only free, it has negative cost; less-free societies forfeit wealth as well as liberty. Increased wealth also tends to increase freedom, not just for individuals but for society as a whole. The freedom of Stone Age people was severely constrained by nature. As civilizations gained greater wealth and autonomy from nature, using science, technology and trade to raise living standards, moral progress became increasingly possible. The expansion of freedom was associated with the expansion of the economy by new economic actors, who demanded liberty and obtained it because they were economically useful. Liberal states rest on a virtuous circle, where greater wealth leads to greater freedom and the ability to spread wealth widely in society; and where greater freedom leads to a more decentralized, creative and wealthy society. Like riding a bicycle, however, the expansion of liberalism requires continued momentum. If society and the economy cannot be improved, the process of mutually reinforcing progress shudders to a halt and goes into reverse. In the Great Depression of 1929–35, wealth was curtailed, and so too was liberty.

While there are some countries outside the West, such as Japan, South Africa, Botswana, and some countries in Latin America, that could be defined in this way as liberal societies, they are few and far between and the permanence of their arrangements cannot be taken for granted.

Many alternatives to liberal civilization are rife outside the West. They comprise personal dictatorship; one-party tyranny; the police and army state; the theocratic state; the 'failed state' sometimes seen in Latin America and Africa, where citizens are prey to crime syndicates, political factions, kidnapping or anarchy; and finally what we may call the quasi-liberal state, where there is formal democracy, a market economy, and the rule of law, but where the habits and ideals of liberalism are not yet fully rooted. The quasi-liberal state has many of the benefits of liberal civilization but lacks at least one of its essentials – full freedom of the individual, equality of status between all citizens, a sense of common identity and membership, freedom of religion, gentle tolerance of minorities, compassion and practical help for weaker members of society, the ability of disparate elements to collaborate effectively, and the ability to survive and replace bad government.

Not only is widespread liberal society uniquely characteristic of the West, it is *universal* within the West and follows a single, common political and social model. There is *one* template for liberty, law, the political process and the protection of human rights, enjoyed by *all* countries of the West. There is *one* political culture, *one* way of life, *one* civilization. This did not arise mechanically or by imposition; it grew from a common history, from a shared set of legal, religious, political, social and economic experiences.

How Western liberal society emerged

The growth of liberty depended on two fortuitous developments – the replacement of feudalism in Europe by the world's first mixed economy between 1000 and 1900; and the invention of modern politics in Europe and America between 1600 and 1900.

Europeans were the first people in the world to escape from the agricultural economy centred on self-sufficient units, the 'manors', which relied upon the use of servile labour, and where the lord of the manor exercised both economic and political control. In the year 1000, this feudal system, which made freedom impossible, was dominant throughout the world. By 1900, uniquely in Europe and countries settled by Europeans, it had utterly gone.

European feudalism retreated for two reasons, the first being the emergence of autonomous city-states in Italy and Holland, and on the Baltic and North Sea coasts. The extent of self-government in these city-states was unprecedented; only the ancient Greek city-states enjoyed anything vaguely comparable, and there were no parallels in the great Asian or Muslim civilizations. Only in European towns did traders, artisans and craftsmen escape feudal restrictions on freedom.[2]

The second liberating development, in late medieval and early modern Europe, was the gradual expansion of 'money agriculture' – growing crops to take to market and exchange for cash, rather than for consumption within the manor. Money agriculture precipitated the slow liquidation of feudal dues and duties, and the acquisition of marketable smallholdings, which turned peasants into small independent farmers ('yeomen'). Money agriculture grew unevenly, flourishing in Holland, England and France before spreading to the rest of Europe.

Trade and money agriculture could not have proliferated had they not been in the economic interests of many, and perhaps most, feudal landowners. This was a story much more of collaboration than of conflict. Merchants need customers. The landowning classes were willing accomplices of the merchants, selling their crops, wool, wood and minerals to them, and buying imports from them – spices, tobacco, exotic goods. As trade and industry grew, so too did the incomes of landowners, and the value of their land. Squires and lords benefited from the expansion of science and technology, of trade, of universities, of royal courts, of manufacturing and mining – from the replacement of feudalism by a more complex and variegated social structure. Where a largely autonomous business class developed first – in Europe as a whole, and especially in England and Holland – it was because the habits of tolerance and reciprocity, of mutual self-interest between different economic groups, and

---

2   See Rosenberg and Birdzell (1986).

of acquiescence in social change because it brought economic benefit, were already widespread.

European governments gradually adjusted to the reality that economic and political concessions to merchants could actually enhance the power and wealth of the state.

In England and Holland, and later elsewhere, rulers gave up the power to confiscate property in return for the right to tax regularly at agreed rates. 'This change had an effect', say economic historians Rosenberg and Birdzell, 'whose significance can be appreciated only by contrast to the Asian and Islamic empires, which never adopted it.'

The invention of modern politics

Rather late in history, in the seventeenth and eighteenth centuries, the West invented modern politics and modern democracy. It happened through five hugely significant, if mainly accidental, political convulsions: the English Revolution of 1640–60, the English Revolution of 1688, the American Revolution of 1776–83, the French Revolution of 1789–94, and the American Civil War of 1861–65.

To be sure, there were earlier ideas and events, all unfolding within Europe, which paved the way for popular politics. Between 6000 and 4000 BCE, the ancient Greeks pioneered democracy, with virtual political equality between citizens, although, of course, excluding the large slave population. Europe also benefited permanently from the great legacy of the Roman Empire – a universal, secular legal system, applied everywhere.

Two developments within Christianity also favoured freedom. First, the Jesus movement grew up as a very small and deviant Jewish sect, dependent for its existence on political toleration and protection by the Roman state. Hence, from the start, the Christians accepted the separation of religion from state authority and the existence of different religious and secular authorities – 'Render to Caesar the things that are Caesar's; and to God the things that are God's.'[3]

Second, the early Christians came up with the most subversive political idea yet to hit the world – that of the equality in Christ of all nations and races, of slaves and masters, and of men and women. The idea that ordinary people mattered and the individual soul had infinite value was peculiarly European; this emphasis was absent in other great religions and cultures, in Islam, in Confucian China, and in Hindu India. There was no parallel either in these civilizations to the extraordinary growth of the cult of the Madonna, the Blessed Virgin, which gradually endowed medieval Europe with a new respect for women.[4]

In 1073, Pope Gregory VII decreed that rulers could be deposed if they defied the will of God. Over the next centuries there were many fierce fights between Church and state. Unwittingly, the pope had opened the door to political pluralism, creating gaps between rival authorities where liberty could nestle.

The Reformation, again unintentionally, greatly facilitated freedom. Martin Luther and John Calvin were not proto-liberals. In Calvin's theocratic state, set up in Geneva in 1541, adulterous men were beheaded, adulterous women were drowned, heretics were burnt alive, and blasphemy and witchcraft were also capital offences. Yet in asserting the rights of the individual to rebel against Europe's supreme cultural and religious authority; in elevating the claims of individual conscience; in by-passing the Catholic

---

3 Matthew 22.21. Philosopher Roger Scruton, in his excellent book about the West and Islam, makes the point that the Christian acceptance of secular law stands in stark contrast to Islam, where 'the legal order is founded in divine commandment'. Muhammad was both a religious and political leader. As a result, states that are not founded on Islamic holy law are not regarded as legitimate. Roger Scruton (2002) *The West and the Rest: Globalization and the Terrorist Threat*, ISI Books, Wilmington/Continuum, London.

4 As historian J. M. Roberts remarks, 'Chaucer's Wife of Bath is not easy to imagine in Ottoman Turkey or Confucian China.' J. M. Roberts (2001) *The Triumph of the West: The Origin, Rise and Legacy of Western Civilization*, Phoenix Press, London.

Church's attempt to stand between God and the individual and in asserting 'the priesthood of all believers'; in moving power from priest to layman; in rejecting the Church's theology, encouraging each Christian to find the truth about God for himself or herself in the Bible; in locating truth in the judgement of ordinary people; in stimulating individualism and autonomous personal responsibility, motivated not by earthly authority but by the desire to attain eternal salvation and avoid eternal damnation; in allowing rulers to use religion as a justification for defying the pope; and in dividing Christendom into states owing allegiance to many different forms of religion, the Reformation had an incalculable effect in stimulating religious pluralism, freedom of thought and political liberty.

Protestantism became the badge of political protest, helping groups such as universities, cities, provinces and parliaments to enlarge their liberties. Colleges and schools set up by the Reformers and counter-Reformers educated many ordinary people and made independent thought possible.

There was an explosion of political theorizing and action in Europe. In the seventeenth century, John Locke (1632–1704) and other thinkers popularized the idea of the 'social contract', that autonomous individuals agreed to come together to form society. The immensity of the Lockean social contract cannot be over-estimated – the state was the servant of the people. Moreover, the ultimate basis of the community, the fundamental particle of society, was the free and independent *individual*.[5]

---

5 The idea of the social contract was given prominence by Thomas Hobbes in *Leviathan*, published in 1651. Paradoxically, Hobbes used the idea to justify a strong state, because (in his account) citizens had chosen to surrender their rights to it, to avoid anarchy. The more natural implication of the social contract, as explicated by Locke and many other writers, was that rights resided with individuals, who decided rationally to combine into civil society. The social contract was probably first invented in the fifteenth century by churchman Jean Gerson. He said that men agreed to pool resources and obey law in the interests of peace; the only legitimate basis of the state was the agreement of citizens.

The revolutionary idea of the social contract could not have triumphed in England without two indispensable developments – the long march of economic progress, and one cataclysmic political event.

In the economic sphere, the key fact was the increasing *interdependence* and *mutual interest* between the old landowning class and the rising 'middle' classes – merchants, small farmers, artisans and craftsmen. The merchants in particular facilitated the 'urbanization of the aristocracy', which brought new wealth and new roles in society to the large landowners.[6] From the sixteenth century to the present day, the English (and later British) Parliament agreed, whether promptly or reluctantly, to every single significant request of the business classes, giving corporations and entrepreneurs increasing autonomy from political and religious interference. By the seventeenth century, and increasingly throughout the next two centuries, the landowners who were dominant in Parliament co-opted the capitalist classes as junior partners in a long series of successful attempts to restrict the arbitrary power of the Crown, making Parliament the supreme arbiter of government and taxation.

The pivotal event, without which liberal society might never have developed anywhere, was the English Revolution of 1640–60. A coalition of dissident gentry, independent farmers, merchants and artisans asserted the supremacy of Parliament, took up arms against the legitimate monarch, defeated his army, executed him and set up a 'Commonwealth' run by Parliament. Although the monarchy was restored in 1660, it was largely on parliamentary sufferance. This was conclusively demonstrated in the 'Glorious Revolution' of 1688. Parliament deposed the Stuart line once and for all, importing William and Mary, liberal and constitutional monarchs from the Netherlands. Before 1776, 'friends of liberty', such as the French Enlightenment philosophers, looked to England as the most politically advanced nation on earth,

---

6   See Rosenberg and Birdzell (1986).

admiring the way that the ruling landowners made astute concessions to the rising middle classes of merchants and industrialists.

The American Revolution of 1776–83 provided an even better
liberal blueprint. The American Constitution was skilfully
designed to pave the way for democracy, while imposing checks
and balances that minimized the risk of violence and tyranny. The
Declaration of Independence, said Thomas Jefferson, would be
'the signal of arousing men to . . . assume the blessings and security
of self-government . . . [based on] the palpable truth that the mass
of mankind has not been born with saddles on their backs, nor a
favored few booted and spurred, ready to ride them'. The
American Revolution, against the British Crown, was the work
very largely of Protestant settlers from Britain. It was wholly in the
tradition of the English Revolutions of 1640 and 1688 – the
assertion of 'no taxation without representation', and British traditions of law, justice, the rights of individuals and of private
property, and restriction of executive power.[7]

America's liberal revolution was completed some 80 years later,
when Abraham Lincoln adroitly associated the North's victory in
the Civil War with a democratic victory over slavery. In the
Gettysburg address in 1863, the President indelibly linked the war
with the promise that 'government of the people, by the people, for
the people, shall not perish from the earth'. The American political
Creed – democracy, equality, non-discrimination, the rights of the
individual, and the decentralization of power – became the gold
standard for liberals everywhere.

By contrast, the French Revolution of 1789–94 stimulated both
democracy and dictatorship, bringing an enduring legacy not just
of 'liberty, equality and fraternity', but of state terror too. The
former legacy was reflected in Napoleon's Civil Code, in the
triumph of constitutional monarchy after the French Revolution
of 1830, and in the Third French Republic from 1871. The

---

7   Excluding Indians and slaves, 80 per cent of the population of the United
    States in 1790 was ethnically British, with the balance being largely German
    and Dutch. Ninety-eight per cent of the white population was Protestant.

bequest of state terror burgeoned in the anti-liberal revolutions of the twentieth century in Russia, Germany, China and many other places.

Twentieth-century threats to liberalism

Since 1900, liberalism and Western liberal society have faced three grave sets of challenges:

1. The threat from *competing ideologies* which had, at times, huge popular support within the West.
2. The threat from *external enemies* linked to ideologies with negligible Western support.
3. Threats from *within Western liberal society* itself.

Competing ideologies

Three ideologies – nationalism, communism and fascism[8] – competed with liberalism for power in the twentieth century.

From the fifteenth century until the nineteenth, *nationalism* slowly incubated in the West. After 1871, for the first time, the boundaries of most Western European states became defined by nationality. Popular nationalism grew apace, fanned by populist authors, newspapers and politicians. Nationalist and racist fervour fuelled the 'expansion of Europe' – the insane age of Imperialism between 1870 and 1914, when most of Africa was seized by

---

8 Strictly speaking, fascism, which was the invention of Mussolini and the ideology governing Italy from 1922 to 1945, should be differentiated from Nazism, the much more virulent and racist force that dominated Germany from 1933 to 1945. In popular usage, however, Nazism is conflated with and included under fascism, and this is good enough for our purposes here. Hitler insisted on rescuing Mussolini's regime when it nearly collapsed. 'After all,' Hitler said, 'it was the Duce who showed us that everything was possible.' As historian Norman Davies remarks, what Mussolini showed to be possible was the subverting of liberal democracy, which in October 1922 made no attempt at all to resist the fascists.

European Powers. An increasingly frantic European arms race followed, culminating in the Great War of 1914–18. The war led to unanticipated and unprecedented carnage, and crushed the West's confident common culture. Virulent nationalism was a key cause of Hitler's rise to power and his near-destruction of Western civilization.

After 1945, rampant nationalism in Europe was eradicated, partly under American sponsorship, by the construction of European economic and political institutions, and the return of prosperity. Never again, it was determined, would European Powers take up arms against each other. The European Union has largely realized this aspiration.[9] Nationalism, a European invention, is still extremely dangerous outside the West. But nationalism no longer threatens the peace or unity of the West or its liberal institutions – a marked advance on the position in 1900.

Like nationalism, *communism* and *fascism* nearly destroyed Western liberal society during the twentieth century. These were internal cancers, incubated within the West. In 1941, communism and fascism had virtually wiped liberalism from the face of continental Europe. North America, Australasia, and for an uncertain duration Great Britain, were almost the sole remnants of Western civilization.

This proved the low point in liberal fortunes. After 1945, fascism as a mass political force disappeared in the West. Communism was imposed on East Germany and most of Central and Eastern Europe, but after 1945 communists never won national elections in any Western country. After the fall of the Berlin Wall in 1989, communism has posed no threat at all to Western liberalism.

---

9 Virulent nationalism has not been totally eradicated from Europe, as the case of Bosnia shows. Nonetheless, harmful European nationalism has been reduced to levels that would have seemed wildly optimistic in 1945.

The threat from external enemies

At times, nationalism, communism and fascism all commanded mass Western support. By contrast, the most significant external threats to the West today have very little popular appeal in the West. The current perils, of course, are various forms of terrorism, and Islamic anti-liberalism, in particular Islamic fundamentalism or 'Islamism'.

How do we assess the threat to the West posed by al-Qa'ida and by other Islamic revolutionaries? The Islamist revolutionary movement is very small and does not represent the great majority of devout Muslims. The threat lies not in the extremists' numbers but in the intensity of their views, and in their support, at various times, by regimes in Iran, Iraq, Libya, Afghanistan, Sudan, Syria, North Korea, and even occasionally by some Western countries. The West's reluctance to support the Palestinian cause increases popular support for the fanatics, who view Western civilization as a form of idolatrous barbarism, which worships not God but money.[10] Bin Laden's assaults on the West are not, however, designed to overturn Western civilization, but rather to encourage the West to stop supporting 'idolatrous' regimes and retreat from the Middle East, and to incite Muslims to overturn those regimes.

The threat from terrorist groups is not new, but the publicity associated with them, and not just with 9/11, can easily make our flesh creep. In 1995, the Japanese sect Aum Shinrikyo – a deviant mix of Hinduism and Buddhism which imagined a global capitalist conspiracy of Jews, Freemasons and Americans – killed 12 people and ruined thousands of other lives by releasing nerve gas into the Tokyo subway. *The Economist* reported that the sect owned a billion dollars and had bought a sophisticated Russian helicopter ready to spray deadly chemicals. Yet even including the bin Laden incidents, the number of international terrorist attacks and their casualties has declined significantly since the mid-1980s.[11]

10 See Ian Buruma and Avishai Margalit (2004) *Occidentalism: A Short History of Anti-Westernism*, Atlantic Books, London.
11 See data from Ferguson (2004), chart on p. 125.

The terrorist threat is clearly real and should not be under-estimated. The West is right to be vigilant; it is impossible to rule out a truly catastrophic terrorist outrage. Measured, however, against the tens of millions killed or enslaved in the last century as a result of nationalism, racism and totalitarian states – tumours from within the West that nearly destroyed Western liberal civil-ization but have now virtually disappeared from the West – contemporary external menaces to liberalism seem almost puny.

Yet the thesis argued by political scientist Francis Fukuyama, that Western liberalism has triumphed perhaps once and for all,[12] does not ring true. Liberalism is much less strongly rooted in Western beliefs and attitudes than it was in 1950 or 1900.

Five self-inflicted threats to liberalism

The most obvious danger is a mutually reinforcing cycle of *terrorism and domestic authoritarianism.* War is the enemy of liberal values. If continual and intensive war is necessary to defeat terrorism and external threats to the West, liberal values will go by the board. The British Labour administration introduced an Anti-Terrorism Act giving it the power to jail citizens indefinitely without charge or trial. Lord Justice Hoffman commented that 'the real threat to the life of the nation, in the sense of a people living in accordance with its traditional laws and political values, comes not from terrorism but from laws such as these'. He was right to do so. Terrorists win when we abandon the very principles of justice and democracy we are seeking to defend.

Terrorists know that illiberal ideas feed on each other, which is why revolutionaries always try to taunt, to encourage ever more extreme reactions. Will the West maintain a sense of proportion, and continue to adhere to liberal values even under severe provoc-ation?

---

12 Francis Fukuyama (1992) *The End of History and the Last Man,* The Free Press, New York.

A related danger comes in the new guise of so-called 'liberal imperialism' – the imposition of democracy by force. Neo-conservatives such as British historian Niall Ferguson argue that many countries would benefit from the imposition of a period of Western rule in order to create a free and democratic society, one that, in Ferguson's words,

> not only underwrites the free international exchange of commodities, labour and capital, but also creates and upholds the conditions without which markets cannot function – peace and order, the rule of law, non-corrupt administration, stable fiscal and monetary policies – as well as provide public goods, such as transport infrastructure, hospitals, and schools . . .[13]

Without the spread of truly deep liberal civilization, he says, the West will never enjoy security. Ferguson points to the successful imposition of democracy on West Germany and Japan after 1945. Who could dispute that it greatly enhanced peace, prosperity and happiness in Germany, Japan and throughout the world?

It is a seductive argument, but not convincing. Leave aside the absurdity of introducing democracy by external force. Reconstructing countries that have been utterly flattened by war, such as Germany and Japan in 1945, where there is no authority, no functioning society, very little food, and no resistance, is not the same as launching a war against a functioning regime. Can war by the West ever be waged in a liberal way? The precedents – from the Boer War, to the firestorms unleashed on Dresden by the RAF and USAF in 1945, to Hiroshima, to Vietnam, to Abu Ghraib and Guantanamo Bay – are not auspicious.[14]

---

13 Niall Ferguson (2004).
14 The terror bombings in Dresden, on the night of 13 February and morning of 14 February 1945, killed at least 120,000 unarmed civilians and refugees, and maybe many more, and destroyed the entire ancient heart of the city. It had almost no military effect. As Germany's President Herzog said in 1995, it was an 'example of the brutalization of man in war'.

Apart from the ethical and historical objections to liberal imperialism, there are two powerful reasons why it won't work. As Niall
Ferguson himself says, an American liberal empire requires a long-
term commitment, to be measured in decades rather than years,
which America is very unlikely to give. 'Despite their country's vast
wealth and lethal weaponry,' says Ferguson, 'Americans have very
little interest in the one basic activity without which a true empire
cannot enduringly be established. They are reluctant to "go there".'
Even when they go, they cannot wait to leave and return to
America. British imperialists were truly engaged by their mission to
spread commerce, Christianity and civilization. 'The contrast with
Americans today', Ferguson continues, 'could scarcely be more
marked.' The United States imports talent; it does not export it.
The American empire, he concludes, 'is not only an empire
without settlers; but also an empire without administrators'.

America, says Ferguson, is 'an empire in denial' which 'tends to
make two mistakes . . . to allocate insufficient resources to the non-
military aspects of the project. The second, and the more serious,
is to attempt economic and political transformation in an unrealis-
tically short time-frame.'

It is worse than Ferguson admits. Liberal imperialism has
immensely harmed America's liberal reputation. The image of the
US outside America – as the great embodiment of freedom and
hope for humankind – has always been one of its great strengths, a
source of 'soft power' for American diplomacy and business alike.
America, as a 'brand', means freedom; its 'logo' is the Statue of
Liberty. 'But today,' says Simon Anholt, a marketing and branding
expert, non-Americans increasingly think that 'America throws its
weight around – culturally, politically, economically and militarily.
And the trouble is that once you start using coercion, persuasion
stops working.'[15] The price of forcibly pushing liberalism is that it
undercuts the powerful pull of liberalism, the attraction of the

15 Simon Anholt (2004) 'Brand America at the Crossroads', in *Critical Eye*,
   December 2004–February 2005, London.

liberal vision for those currently outside its domain. Any astute marketeer knows that ultimately pull works better than push.

If the first two threats to liberalism, anti-terrorism and 'liberal' imperialism, are substantially at the West's discretion, the third is more difficult to avoid or counter. It lies in the *fragmentation and devaluation of the political process*. The invention of modern politics, with its parliaments, parties and mass engagement of citizens in politics, was an essential step in the construction of liberal civilization. Now, the political underpinnings of liberalism are being nibbled away. Liberal democracy requires an important political stage; and a large and appreciative audience, one· that participates enthusiastically in politics.

But the trend in society is to reposition the stage, to move the spotlight from elected chamber to television studio, and from serious issues of policy and government to the trivia of personalities and scandal. Political communication now belongs to the media, a space irretrievably denied to governments and oppositions who, when they try to counter spin with spin, inevitably appear debased and petty. Now that social and economic classes are more heterogeneous and less important, the party system is in danger of losing its appeal and resonance. The instinctive class-based appeal of traditional parties has waned. Where there is passionate interest in political ideas – as with many young people's concern about globalization, environmental damage, fair trade and developing country debt – it usually fails to be reflected in the priorities of mainstream politics.

As society becomes more pluralistic, and the claims of global reach and local identity reinforce each other, power increasingly resides everywhere and nowhere. The vigor of the national state and national bureaucracy has been eroded. Political excitement belongs to mavericks and 'personalities', new stars whom the media delight in catapulting to brief fame and then snuffing out. It is not surprising that polls everywhere in the West show that public respect for politicians and trust in government has declined dramatically since the 1960s.

The fourth problem for liberalism is its increasing *divorce from its ethical base*, the weakening commitment to community, and the lack of real passion on the part of liberals. Liberalism was an offshoot of Jewish and Christian beliefs. The most successful societies and elements in society are those that combine liberalism with a belief that humanity's purpose lies beyond material gratification. People and societies thrive when they believe in some cause beyond self-advancement. Even business corporations need a cause outside themselves in order to flourish.

Initially, liberals found an exciting cause in liberalism itself – in crusades for the abolition of slavery; for the extension of the vote lower down the social scale, then for universal male suffrage, and finally for votes for all women; for ending discrimination against Catholics, Jews, blacks and homosexuals; for the abolition of corporal and capital punishment and for penal reform; for the protection of workers and their trade unions; for action to mitigate or substantially remove the scourges of hunger and unemployment; for universal education; for the provision of health insurance or socialized medicine; for the right of women to control their own bodies; and for the re-distribution of income.

In this light, liberals were as effective in the twentieth century as they were in the nineteenth. Not all liberal causes have been fully successful, but the major battles have long been fought and won in most Western countries. Yet the substantial triumph of liberalism has narrowed the appeal of liberalism and doused its fire. Then there is the impact of the new personalized economy. There is now little to differentiate the economic policies of liberal socialists (outside France and Germany, at least) from conservatives, as the former have embraced market forces and conceded the limited efficacy of high taxation. Most liberals have ceded this ground for very good economic and electoral reasons, but in doing so have forfeited part of the emotional appeal of liberalism from Benjamin Franklin to J. K. Galbraith – a deep commitment to protect and help the poorer sections of society.

What is most noteworthy, however, is the increasing moral

emptiness of liberalism, its lack of high ideals and the emotional void at its heart. The seeds of liberalism's downfall lie in its success. To come to full fruition, liberalism has to create a rich, complex and highly social society. Liberalism is more than national autonomy, more than democracy, more than a thriving set of political ideas, institutions and parties, more than the rule of law, and more than habits of honesty in business and administration. All of these qualities are essential for vibrant liberalism. But at its zenith, liberal society also depends on community spirit, on a set of common assumptions about the virtues of a tolerant and humane way of life, a common identity and equality of status for all citizens, on the value of knowledge and reason, on the importance of fairness, and on the merits of a pluralistic, varied, and decentralized culture.

Self-governing societies need strong bonds of trust and respect between citizen and citizen, between citizen and public institutions, and between ordinary citizens and elites of all kinds, and between the various elites. Different elements of society, and different Western countries, will not – should not – think alike, but if liberal civilization is to work properly there must be mutual respect and a sense of underlying common identity and purpose. In a decentralized world, enlightened self-interest does not provide this bonding. Intense belief in the virtues of liberalism becomes more difficult as liberal societies mature, grow more complex and prosperous, and as citizens forget what it took to build such cultures in the first place. The sense of common association wanes. The wealthiest and most pluralistic societies are those most prey to vacuous consumerism and cynicism about the common good. In some of the most advanced liberal societies, conspicuously of course in America, the problem is compounded when the law, hitherto a guarantee of fairness and equality between citizens, is used to extort money from fellow citizens.

Finally, there is liberalism's *internal compulsion toward self-destruction*. Taken to an illogical but emotionally gratifying extreme, liberalism denies its own superiority. The quest for precise equality of outcome can destroy equality of opportunity. While the battle against inequality remains a key cause for most liberals, it can easily slip into suppressing individuality. A mistaken belief in the 'politically correct' tends to ignore uncomfortable results of scientific research, especially in psychology and biology.

Most importantly, the denial of authority can engender subjective sterility, where any point of view appears as good as another. Postmodern philosophers assert that everything is relative. Truth becomes 'privatized', a matter of personal opinion rather than a matter of importance arrived at by scientific investigation and public debate. Not only is nothing better than anything else, but also we can never know the nature of truth.[16] This dubious philosophy has been used to justify ignorance and elevate emotion and opinion above reason and science.

Relativism corrodes the sense of responsibility without which liberal society cannot work. Reasoned debate can only impose obligations on members of society if they acknowledge that there is such a thing as 'the public good' and that some policies and some forms of behaviour are better than others.

The sense of personal responsibility is also being undermined by another development. Increasingly, personal disadvantages, or the defects of society, are regarded as an excuse for antisocial behaviour. Whole swathes of Western society have come to see themselves as 'victims' who are therefore not liable for the consequences of their actions. The mass manufacture of 'victims' has done untold damage both to them and to the sense of citizens' mutual responsibility that liberal communities require. History furnishes countless examples where the human spirit has overcome war, disability, plague, oppression, famine, flood, poverty, social discrimination, and even concentration camps. It is insulting to

---

16 For a fair-minded examination of relativism, see Simon Blackburn (2005) *Truth: A Guide for the Perplexed*, Penguin, London. As he says, 'It is this privatisation of belief that leads to relativism: my belief ceases to exist in a public space, up for acceptance or rejection by all who pay attention. It starts to be a matter of "my truth" or "your truth" . . . This is not how we need to think of beliefs' (p. 9).

assume that disadvantaged people cannot rise above their tribulations, that the suffering and difficulties of all human life somehow justify antisocial or criminal activity. Liberal civilization – in both its Anglo-Saxon and social-democratic guises – rests on overcoming problems and bad behaviour, not multiplying them; on taking responsibility, not denying it.[17]

Indiscriminate respect for all cultures, all peoples and all views shades into acceptance of anti-intellectualism and anti-liberalism. If everything is relative, then anything – cannibalism, genocide – can be justified. Liberals can be soft touches. An attempt to see all points of view, filtered through the liberal mind, can lead to a belief that if fanatics such as suicide bombers hate us, then we must have done something terrible to generate this hatred. That way lies our own suicide – if fascist enemies cannot be recognized, and if liberals will not fight for liberal values, then the barbarians will win. Many Western liberals are perversely unwilling to recognize the unprecedented virtues of Western liberal society – something that other societies could not have produced, something that is worth defending and, by mutual consent, extending. Perversely, the most dangerous enemy of liberalism is liberalism.

Conclusion

Though Westerners rarely acknowledge it, Western liberal civilization provides far greater benefits for its citizens than other civilizations. Liberal society is the most successful formula yet devised, and probably that could ever be devised, for combining a vibrant and dynamic economy and society with the highest ideals of human dignity and autonomy.

The West is unique in having, in all its countries, with their differing and ever-changing political complexions, one common political and social culture, that of liberal civilization. While liberal

---

17 See Yvonne McEwan, 'Manufacturing Victims', *LM*, March 1999, pp. 18–19.

societies exist outside the West, the norm is quasi-liberal states, failed states or tyranny.

Liberalism is the theory and practice of freedom. Freedom arose as a result of unique European and American historical developments, notably the influence of Christianity and of radical, egalitarian ideas; the struggle for political rights by self-confident and economically important individuals and groups; and the development of habits of collaboration across groups and classes, fuelled by increasing wealth.

It is more difficult for countries outside the West to develop liberal civilization, simply because their history is different from that of Europeans and Americans. Other countries need to go through a long period of struggle and constructive conflict, including the evolution of collaboration between different social groups, if democracy and freedom are to mean anything when they arrive. It is possible that the pressures of globalization and the arrival of instant pre-packaged Western mores may deny many non-Western countries the time and isolation necessary to develop their own viable liberal societies. Of course, those outside the West may develop even better polities and societies, building on or independent of Western models; but the early signs are not auspicious. If better models are not developed, the best that can be hoped for may be somewhat inauthentic imitations of Western liberalism that nonetheless work tolerably well.

In the twentieth century, Western liberalism was nearly killed off by challenges from three competing Western ideologies – nationalism, fascism and communism. The current external threats to liberalism – revolutionary Islam and many other strains of terrorism – have little popular appeal in the West and are militarily weak.

Yet despite its success, and the weakness of its external enemies, liberal civilization is under dire threat. The most serious dangers are all self-inflicted. Although the liberal agenda in the last century has been marvellously effective in increasing the security, welfare and freedom of ordinary Westerners, liberalism is much less appreciated than it used to be. Liberalism arose because of the West's history, but history alone cannot sustain liberalism. It needs constant practice and renewal.

'Liberal imperialism' has tarnished America's global image as the home of freedom. The media have usurped and diminished the political stage; politics has become trivialized and devalued. Liberals have lost self-confidence, passion and forward momentum. Most harmfully, the dogma of relativism has manufactured millions of anti-social 'victims', removing the sense of civic responsibility without which liberal communities cannot thrive. The devaluation and privatization of truth is profoundly dangerous, because ultimately a civilization requires a set of shared beliefs that underpin confident, collaborative action.

Unless enthusiastic liberals – of all political parties and persuasions, and none – stand up for collaborative freedom and rekindle enthusiasm for it, the West is likely to move to a less pleasant civilization, where liberty and community fade because there is no inspiring cause to lift citizens above the relentless pursuit of self-interest.

7 Individualism

If there is one defining quality of the West, which its protagonists and antagonists agree is central to its character, it is individualism. The rise and rise of individualism is *the* motif running through Western history, from Christianity, to the Renaissance, the Reformation, and the growth of the modern economy and modern society. Western individualism has no similar roots in any other civilization. Even cultures permeated by Western ideas and Western business practice, such as those of Japan, Korea, Singapore and Hong Kong, have not become individualistic in the Western way. All the enemies of American–European civilization in the twentieth century – the communists, the Nazis, Imperial Japan and extreme Islamic groups – have hated Western individualism with utter passion and conviction, and sought to provide alternative bases of identity and commitment. Those within the West who have doubts about their own culture usually single out individualism – with its attendant selfishness, alienation and divisiveness – as the root cause of the problem.

Nobody believes that Western individualism is weak or in danger. There are rather two issues: the type and moral nature of the individualism that prevails; and whether it is harmful or beneficial.

The origins of individualism

The ancient Greeks probably invented individualism. Nine or eight centuries before Christ, the *Odyssey* and the *Iliad* describe gods and humans who clearly had individual characteristics. But it was the Hebrews who made individualism the right and responsibility, not just of heroes and gods, but of ordinary people too.

The Jewish prophets, in the 500 years before Christ, individualized morality. They preached not just to the Hebrew leaders, but to ordinary people as well, appealing to a sense of conscience and compassion that, they felt, could live within everyone.

The words attributed to Christ by the Gospel writers, and the message indelibly stamped on Christianity by St Paul, left no doubt about the worth of each individual in the sight of God, and the individual's responsibility to improve himself or herself.

In Christ, Paul claimed, the 'new Adam', a new and improved human prototype, could flourish – a higher self, 'no longer I, but Christ in me'. Paul described his own mental torment, the fight between Christ and the Devil, within his own inner depths. Over the next few centuries, Christian theologians agreed that every human possessed an immortal and infinitely valuable soul.

The idea that every individual has personality, inner depths and a 'self' securely embedded within the world is so fundamental to Western identity as to seem obvious, yet this self-awareness did not exist before Christianity, and only became fully developed in the last thousand years. As Canadian philosopher Charles Taylor says, 'We naturally come to think that we have selves the way we have heads or arms, and inner depths the way we have hearts or livers', but pre-Christian humanity did not have this sense at all.[1] The origin of individuality was religious, and specifically it was Christian – based on the idea that God could live within individuals and endow their actions with sacred significance. 'God is the light of my heart', said St Augustine, 'and the bread that nourishes my soul, and the power which weds my mind to my inmost thoughts.'

---

1 Charles Taylor (1989) *Sources of the Self: The Making of the Modern Identity*, Cambridge University Press, Cambridge.

Historians generally place the full development of the idea of personality in the period between 1000 and 1500. In 1918, Oswald Spengler drew attention to the uniquely European cult of personality and to its medieval religious roots:

> The coming of this specific 'I' is the first dawning of that personality-idea which was so much later to create the sacrament of Contrition and *personal* absolution . . . Western man lives in the *consciousness* of his becoming and his eyes are constantly upon past and future . . . No [ancient] Greek would have been capable of a genuine self-criticism . . . There is nothing so impersonal as Greek art . . .
>
> It is the fundamental postulate of our ethical systems . . . that man has character, *the personality, the relation of living to doing* . . . The conception of mankind as an active, fighting, progressing whole is . . . so necessary an idea for us that we find it hard indeed to realize that it is an exclusively Western hypothesis, living and valid only for a season . . .[2]

Personality was implicit in the earliest Christian teaching, but was brought into sharper relief between 1050 and 1200. Peter Watson gives three possible causes for the growth in individuality:

1. The growth of cities and secular professions such as the law, business and teaching.
2. The growth in primogeniture, which gave land to the first-born and required younger sons to seek their fortune in individualized pursuits.
3. The rediscovery of classical antiquity, which showed ancient authorities disagreeing among themselves and taking a different line from that of the Church.[3]

---

2 Spengler (1991): 'What happened to Oedipus – unlike the fate of Lear – might just as well have happened to anyone else. This is the Classical [ancient Greek] "Destiny", the *Fatum* which is common to all mankind, which . . . in no wise depends upon incidents of personality.'

3 Watson (2005).

Probably most important was the idea of *individual faith*: 'Know yourself as a way to God.'[4] From the twelfth and thirteenth centuries, the battle between God and the Devil assumed new prominence, leading to 'ceaseless mine-warfare within the self'.[5] Before 1200, the practice of confession was rare, but in 1215 the Fourth Lateran Council required everyone to confess at least once a year, preferably much more often. Contrition is something that the *individual* accomplishes *alone*. The invention of commercial printing in 1457 and the consequent spread of silent reading reinforced introspection and a sense of interior individuality.[6]

Thus the Renaissance did not discover personality, but it did project it to the surface of society, where it became visible to everyone. Especially in art, there was an explicit recognition of human beings as *individual people* – not just ciphers or symbols. It was the moment in cultural and intellectual history when 'humanness' was first fully embraced.

The three greatest Renaissance figures – Leonardo, Raphael and Michelangelo – were not just artists but thinkers and scientists, restless polymaths trying every means of self-expression and self-discovery available, men with impossibly high ambitions, forever trying to release humankind from its earthly shackles. It was no accident that Leonardo tried to invent flying machines and also portrayed angels and saints floating luxuriantly in space, free of terrestrial cares.[7] Imagination, ambition and achievement supplanted noble blood as the focus of social admiration and, very often, the

---

4 Robert Benson and Giles Constable (eds) *Renaissance and Renewal in the Twelfth Century* (1991) Oxford University Press, Oxford.

5 Spengler (1991).

6 The first printed book using moveable type that can be dated was the *Mainz Psalter* of 14 October 1457. Publishers (printers) were particularly partial to promoting heresy, since, then as now, scandal created publicity and bestsellers.

7 This point is well made by Spengler (1991): 'To fly, to free oneself from earth, to lose oneself in the expanse of the universe – is this not Faustian in the highest degree? Is it not in fact the fulfilment of our dreams? . . . the insistent emphasis upon freedom from earth's heaviness, are emblems of soul-flight, peculiar to the art of the Faustian, utterly remote from that of the Byzantine.'

road to riches. The long process whereby individuality came to trump aristocracy had begun to roll.

The Reformation reinforced individualism in many profound and unintended ways: in the sheer audacity of one individual challenging Christendom's most prestigious and holy institution; in asserting the claims of individual conscience against authority; in claiming 'the priesthood of all believers', the possibility of each individual establishing an intimate relationship with God, cutting out the Church, breaking its monopoly of God and theology, and eliminating the hierarchical distinction between cleric and layman; in erecting competing churches and allowing rulers and subjects to make a choice between them, thus paving the way for religious pluralism, and ultimately for scepticism and atheism. To be sure, Lutheranism and Calvinism at their fiercest were intolerant creeds, throwbacks to primitive, Judaic Christianity, based more on fear than love. But like the Christian fundamentalists of our own time, their attempts to discipline and constrain individuals were inconceivable without the prior progress of individualism, enabling Luther, Calvin, John Knox and other evangelists to revolt against established authority and assert their individual visions.

As Max Weber wrote 100 years ago, Luther invented the idea of a 'calling', 'the valuation of the fulfilment of duty in world affairs as the highest form which the moral activity of the individual could assume'.[8] Calvin added to this 'the idea of the necessity of proving one's worth in worldly activity', as a sign that one belonged to the elect and not the damned.

With Protestant religion, therefore, autonomy is not merely grasped by the individual; in a paradoxical but very important sense, it is *imposed on* the individual. Weber claimed that the identification of personal responsibility with diligent money-making left an indelible mark on Western civilization and hastened the spread of capitalism, by encouraging frugality, saving and personal striving in business. Weber's thesis is still controversial. But what is

---

8   Weber (1985).

absolutely clear is that Luther and Calvin *did* preach a new sense of personal responsibility in daily business affairs, and that this influenced millions of individuals, eventually transmuting into the dominant business ethic of America and much of Europe, an ethic clearly derived from religious motives but, already by the time of the American Revolution, largely independent of them.[9]

What Weber did not note was that his 'spirit of capitalism' actually pre-dated not only industrial capitalism, but also the Reformation, by several centuries. As already shown, medieval Europe, from the early eleventh century, was unique in developing independent city-states that harboured a new class of free and autonomous traders, merchants, craftsmen and artisans, often gaining strength from organization into guilds, collective bodies of individuals. Europe was also the first region of the world to loosen the shackles tying peasants to the land. In some countries – especially Holland and England – many peasants were able to become small landholders, responsible for their own living rather than being serfs on their lord's manor.

A more plausible alternative to Weber's thesis that Protestantism led to capitalism is that capitalism – if by that we mean free market activity – led to Protestantism. The free market niches of Europe, populated by serious, independent, self-employed individuals, provided a receptive audience for the message of Luther and Calvin.

---

9 Weber has great fun quoting Franklin's *Advice to a Young Tradesman* (1784), perhaps the first modern self-help book, which contains such gems as 'Remember, that *time* is money . . . Remember that *credit* is money . . . money can beget money, and its offspring can beget more, and so on . . . He that murders a crown [five shillings, a quarter of a pound sterling], destroys all that it might have produced, even scores of pounds . . . The sound of your hammer at five in the morning, or eight at night, heard by a creditor, makes him easy six months longer; but if he sees you at a billiard-table, or hears your voice at a tavern, when you should be at work, he sends for his money the next day. . .' As Weber remarks, this is religious ideology now stripped of religious motive and inculcated for its own value: 'all Franklin's moral attitudes are coloured with utilitarianism. Honesty is useful, because it assures credit; so are punctuality, industry, frugality . . .'

However this may be, Europe, and later America, were undoubtedly the first places on earth to be home to hundreds of thousands, and then millions, of people, and a significant proportion of the population, who were, quite consciously, economically independent, interested in advancing their political liberty, and endowed with a strong sense of personal responsibility and personal striving. Many also made a point of consciously choosing their own religion. Economic, political, religious and intellectual autonomy were painfully gained and greatly cherished by generations of these people.

The spirit of individualism which grew out of the economic, religious and political milieu and history of Europe and America is, quite naturally and inevitably, deeper, more entrenched, and more pervasive, than that felt or experienced by any other civilization.

If we have lost sight of this rather obvious truth, it is because there is a tendency to believe that individualism is the product of the last century, or of neo-conservative ideology, or of the consumer society. Actually individualism evolved slowly over more than 2,000 years, and is the complex product of unique developments in European and American thought and history.

We can trace the sense of the unfolding of inner potential in the ideas developed by Michel de Montaigne (1533–92) and René Descartes (1596–1650). In an essay published in 1580, Montaigne provided a startlingly modern justification of individualism:

> The greatest thing on earth is to know how to belong to oneself. Everybody looks in front of them. But I look inside myself. I have no concerns but my own. I constantly reflect on myself; I control myself; I taste myself . . . We owe some things to society, but the greater part to ourselves. It is necessary to lend oneself to others, but to give oneself only to oneself.[10]

---

10 Michel de Montaigne (1580) *Essais*, quoted by Norman Davies (1996) *Europe: A History*, Oxford University Press, Oxford, p. 483.

Descartes firmly located moral authority and self-sufficiency *within* the individual. 'Free will is the noblest thing we can have,' he told Queen Christina of Sweden, 'because it makes us in a certain manner equal to God and exempts us from being his subjects.' For the first time, the individual is *required* to create and originate his or her own philosophy of life. Descartes' famous observation, 'I think, therefore I am', implies the 'thinking self', the rational individual.

The later intellectual development of individualism is well known. In the seventeenth century, John Locke said human reason was the sole way to appreciate reality. Both English Revolutions of 1640 and 1688 were the result *and* the cause of a wave of radical political theorizing, notably the rejection of arbitrary royal authority and the rights of citizens, praising and reinforcing the 'sturdy independence' and dignity of the yeomen (small farmers). 'Enlightenment' philosophers followed up with theories of the 'social contract', 'the liberty of the individual', and 'human rights', making the individual the source of all legitimate authority, and human happiness the measure of public policy. Immanuel Kant (1724–1804) developed a theory of secular morality, where citizens have mutual rights and obligations, and where the innate soul of the individual, with its own distinct identity, finds its full expression in relationships with other individuals.

Charles Taylor describes how from this time 'a new moral culture radiates outward and downward from the upper middle classes of England, America, and (for some facets) France . . . a culture which is individualist in three senses: it prizes autonomy; it gives an important place to self-exploration, in particular of feeling; and its vision of the good life generally involves personal commitment' to causes and other people.

Individualism was given a distinctive twist by Romantic writers – notably Jean-Jacques Rousseau (1712–78), Johann Gottfried von Herder (1744–1803), and, in his earlier career, Johann Wolfgang von Goethe (1749–1832). The Romantics portrayed nature as benign, nurturing a relationship with humanity. Individuals could immerse themselves in nature, to reach new depths of feeling and self-expression. Romanticism added to individualism the notion of originality – every single person alive has some incomparable, inimitable and unrepeatable expression of life, and human destiny lies in fulfilling our originality. The Romantics were responsible for the uniquely elevated view that Western civilization gives to artists and creative imagination.

Along with liberalism and nationalism, individualism became the dominant ideology of the nineteenth century. Individualism was closely associated with liberalism and with the great campaigns of *human benevolence and universal justice* – in England, for example, with the successful crusade in abolishing the slave trade in 1807 and slavery itself in 1833. In the twentieth century, all the ideals advancing human dignity, relieving suffering and eroding hierarchies and artificial distinctions between people, are the culmination of individualism, the belief in the sacred nature and rights of every human being.

In the years straddling the end of the nineteenth century and the start of the twentieth, a new philosophy of society and government emerged, that of democratic socialism. It was based on the insight that the well-being of *society* and the fulfilment of every *individual* within society are wholly interdependent. Democratic socialism held that individuals benefited from pooling some of their freedom and resources as part of a common endeavour to advance human dignity and equality. It drew much of its strength and vitality from the development of trades unions, cooperatives and 'friendly societies', in which individuals combine together to achieve greater advancement of their individual goals than they could by acting alone, without in any way sacrificing their personal identity and sense of self-worth. Over the past hundred years, this blend of democracy, socialism and individualism has been most influential in Western Europe. On the whole, democratic socialism has worked remarkably well in protecting the social fabric and maintaining social stability, while enhancing individual freedom in a way that state-socialist and other centralized societies never attempted.

In the early twentieth century, many observers, right across the political spectrum, forecast that collectivist philosophies would utterly replace individualism. Oswald Spengler saw executive power passing 'to new forces – party leaders, dictators, presidents, prophets and their adherents – towards which the multitude continues to be unconditionally the passive object'. Dictators duly strutted on to the stage. Yet, as the twentieth century rolled on, individualism became ever more deeply rooted in Europe and America, acquiring an often radical and youth-oriented aspect that moved well beyond traditional 'bourgeois' values. Material plenty, a huge increase in the numbers of students, and the relaxation of authority's constraints on individuals triggered new phenomena – night clubs, movie stars, jazz, rhythm and blues, the teenager, pop music, millionaire adolescent pop stars, the rebel without a cause, the beatnik, the mod, the rocker, the hippy, psychedelic drugs, the student revolutions of 1968–69 with their strong undercurrent of sexual liberation, a mass feminist movement, gay and lesbian liberation, rock music, radical environmentalists, the populist billionaire entrepreneur, sports stars, punk music and fashion, designer drugs, house music, and a kaleidoscope of other global fads and identities. Nearly all were libertarian, originating in America or Europe before spreading around the world. Never in human history has it been easier – indeed, almost mandatory – to do one's own thing.

Some of these colourful phenomena were transient, even fleeting. Others, however, stayed the course and changed society. What makes the continuing crescendo of individualism almost inevitable in the West is the translation of creative revolt from American and European campuses to the business arena. There we find new and rapidly growing creative industries – art, design, consulting, communications, movies, music, software, biotechnology and many others – where human imagination creates wealth. The most important economic trend, accelerating since 1950, has been the invention and decentralization of information technology, together with a vast new wave of entrepreneurial activity built around and benefiting individual innovators.

Divergent thinking, a strong dash of iconoclastic revolt, and limitless imagination are the drivers of business success. Divergent thinking results in divergent product categories, divergent brands, divergent ways of doing business, and colossal personal success for innovators. The transistor, the microchip, the microprocessor, the *personal* computer, innovative software, the Internet, personalized devices of all kinds, and the relentless pursuit of technological *and* non-technological breakthroughs, all are manifestations of the spirit of revolt and a new individualized world, where the expansion of the human mind drives not only personal fulfilment but also new industries, new ways of doing business, and breathtaking personal enrichment. If there is one single, ever more powerful, trend driving individualism in the West, it is the personalization of business and business success. Through a combination of cultural and economic forces, individualism has taken the West to a totally new experience – the *personalized society*.

The West is different

Anthropologist Richard Shweder, who has studied moralizing across all cultures, explains that there is a fundamental difference between Western and non-Western concepts of fundamental morality. Non-Western traditions, he says, have rich theories of moralizing, but they are based either on the ethic of *community* – the norms of the social group, laden with values such as duty, respect, deference and adherence to convention – or else on the ethic of *divinity*, the purity and holiness required by God. By contrast, Shweder says, Westerners tend to frame moral judgements in terms of *autonomy*, which he defines as the individual's rights and interests. In the West, fairness to every individual is the cardinal virtue.[11]

One of the most thoughtful scholars to devote his life to studying values in different countries is Dutch sociologist Geert Hofstede. His magisterial study of cultural attitudes among IBM employees in 53 countries defines four attributes that differ markedly according to nationality:

1. Power distance (the perception of equality or inequality of personal status).
2. Uncertainty avoidance.
3. Masculinity versus femininity.
4. Individualism as opposed to collectivism.

Western countries are most clearly different from non-Western countries on the dimension of individuality. The most individualistic countries are the United States, Australia and Great Britain, with Canada, The Netherlands and New Zealand not far behind. Western countries take the top 20 slots in degree of individualism, with an average score among all Western countries of 66.7.[12] By contrast, the average score for all non-Western countries is just 25.7.[13]

According to Hofstede, the dilemma for non-Western countries is clear. They must either change their cultural assumptions – which he says is difficult, if not impossible – or fall behind in relative prosperity:

---

11 R. A. Shweder, N. C. Much, M. Mahapatra and L. Park: 'The "big three" of morality and the "big three" of suffering', in A. Brandt and P. Rozin (eds), *Trends in Cognitive Science* (1997) Nova Science Publishers, St Louis, Mo., pp. 296–301. Of course, not all Western thinkers elevate individual fairness so high. For example, Jeremy Bentham advocated 'the greatest happiness of the greatest number' and Kant placed duty above fairness.

12 The lowest scoring Western countries were Turkey (37), Greece (35) and Portugal (27). Excluding these scores the average Western score was 71.8. The top five were the United States (91), Australia (90), Great Britain (89), Canada (80) and The Netherlands (80).

13 Hofstede (2001).

The evidence showed that there was no international convergence of cultural values over time, except towards increased individualism for countries having become richer.[14] Value differences between nations described centuries ago are still present today, in spite of close contacts. For the next few hundred years, countries will remain culturally very diverse.

A popular business slogan is: 'Think globally, act locally.' To me this phrase is both naïve and arrogant. No one, as this book has amply proven, can think globally. We all think according to our local software.

Psychologist Richard Nisbett has studied Western and Eastern patterns of thought and concluded that they have been and remain fundamentally distinct:

East and West are in general quite different from each other with regard to a great many centrally important values and social-psychological attributes ... Differences between Easterners and Westerners have been found in virtually every study we have undertaken and they are usually large.[15]

---

14 There could, of course, be a debate about what is cause and what is effect. It is possible, for instance, that as non-Western countries become richer, they will also become more individualistic, even though this has not happened yet to any marked degree, as Hofstede's data indicate. But he comments: 'We have seen that individualism was strongly correlated with wealth (1970 GDP *per capita*). Across 50 countries the correlation coefficient was a striking r = .84 . . . Poverty makes people depend on the support of their in-groups, but when a country's wealth increases, its citizens get access to resources that allow them to "do their own thing" . . . Collective life is replaced by individual life.' We are not convinced. The correlation, which is at one point in time rather than across time, may be somewhat specious, because the richest countries were both Western and individualistic. In part at least, we argue that rich countries are rich *because* they are individualistic (and they are individualistic more because they are Western than because they are rich), a trend that is becoming increasingly important as the personalized economy burgeons. See Chapter 5.

15 Nisbett (2003).

He points out that despite modernization and the adoption of Western economic systems, 'there are numberless signs that Japan has changed little in many social respects and we find large differences between the way Japanese and Westerners perceive the world'.

The problem with the personalized society

The problem with the personalized society is that it erodes community, while increasing the stress on individuals. Traditional, more centralized societies give less freedom to individuals but also require less from them by way of thought or original contribution. A centralized world works through institutions, power relationships, well-defined roles and various forms of community identity. The individual's identity comes from sharing in a number of overlapping collective groupings – nation, class, school, organization, trade union, profession, church, political party, voluntary group, extended family, locality. Everyone has clear obligations to these groups, which take upon themselves the burden of defining behaviour and expectations. In a centralized society, the individual does what he or she is told, and though the person may not like it, there is little leeway for angst, self-doubt, depression or anti-social behaviour. In practice, most people in centralized societies conform to their roles with a willing heart, even to the extent of laying down their lives in war.

The personalized society is quite different. In his compelling book, *Bowling Alone*, Harvard professor Robert D. Putnam shows how 'social capital' is destroyed as society becomes more individualistic and we become disconnected from family, friends, neighbours, clubs, churches, associations and community groups. Trust, an important ingredient of psychological health and of economic success, breaks down as we become strangers to one another.[16]

---

16 Robert D. Putnam (2000) *Bowling Alone: The Collapse and Revival of American Community*, Simon & Schuster, New York.

But the fragmentation of society, the destruction of social capital and the collapse of community feeling is only half the problem. The other half is greatly enhanced personal responsibility and anxiety. Life becomes more difficult.

The personalized society brings freedom, but it requires hard choices that previously were prescribed or automatic – what education to commit to, what career to pursue, what kind of personal relationship to have, whether to maintain or jettison that relationship, where to live, what friends to cultivate, and what kind of person to become. The personalized society brings unprecedented opportunity, but greatly increases the possibility of personal failure, the sense of being left behind and rejected. The personalized society brings wealth for many, but turns the gap between winners and losers into a yawning chasm. The sky is the limit but there are no alibis for plunging to earth. Every society has had self-made individuals, but only modern Western society has multitudes of self-destroyed people. For every winner, it seems, there have to be several losers.

It is not hard to grasp why individualism, at its moment of greatest triumph, is so unpopular, not least among most Western intellectuals. Individuals are enjoying ever greater personal freedom, yet feeling ever greater discomfort with it. Whether from guilt at success (an astounding proportion of 'successful' people now say they feel unhappy, unfulfilled or even failures), or from excuses for failure, we are not enjoying our expanded personal responsibility. Western countries with the highest degree of individual liberty and modernity also exhibit soaring incidence of the victim mentality, of depression and suicide, alienation, narcissism, selfishness, lack of purpose, nostalgia, proliferating envy, collapsing social capital and retreat into authoritarian religious sects.

Above all, the personalized society is disliked because of accelerating inequality. When individuals are able to create great wealth, and to keep most of what they create, inequality inevitably multiplies.

Can the personalized society work?

Yes, it can. Here are four reasons why.

First, the personalized society represents but the latest and most highly developed form of a process that has been going on, with two steps forward and one step back, for a very long time. For the last thousand years, Western civilization has progressively evolved greater and greater degrees of freedom and autonomy for the individual. Every time social constraints have been relaxed, the cry has gone up that this is too much, that the outcome will be anarchy, devastation and the destruction of civilization itself. And the path to freedom *has* been rocky and at times extremely perilous for the orderly working of society. Peasant revolts; the burning of tens of thousands of witches; religious persecution and wars; civil wars; the appalling terror of the French Revolution; two terrible world wars, which started as European civil wars; the even more horrific tyrannies of Stalin, Hitler and Mao Zedong – all derived partly from the quest for liberty and the reaction against it.

There was absolutely no inevitability in the transition from feudalism to capitalism to the personalized society, in the relatively happy outcome of the West's pluralistic, wealthy and free society. There is no guarantee that the West will not relapse into barbarism, fascism or some other form of authoritarian rule, or be overcome by enemies bent on tyranny and social control.

Yet, seen in its long history, the progressive development and exercise of freedom in the West has faced and survived far worse crises than any apparent today. The patchwork quilt of modern identity, and the multiplication of sources of power among many institutions and individuals, are symptoms not of society gone awry but of a coming to terms with a new freedom – the genuine autonomy of the individual. When social controls on millions of people are relaxed, it is certain that some of them will abuse or cope badly with their new independence. In the bad old days, people did what they were told. Now they can misbehave – and many do, but far more don't. Freedom is generally exercised maturely, because most people realize that the quality of society and their own happiness depend upon behaving responsibly, upon collaborating with other free individuals. Ultimately, responsible individualism can produce a stronger and more genuine sense of community than that previously foisted upon citizens by higher authority. 'Trust the people!' It has worked before.

Second, Western society is in transition from a sense of community built on automatic social and institutional foundations to one of community built on individually constructed *reciprocity* and on a sense of common identity that we call *virtual reciprocity*. Reciprocity means that I behave reasonably, collaboratively and generously, because I know that this is the way to induce you to behave back to me in the same terms. Reciprocity, a compound of affection and calculation, has always stood at the root of all friendships and most human relationships, but increasingly it provides the basis for every civilized community. Now that organizations can no longer regulate behaviour as effectively as they did, individuals have to regulate themselves. And since reciprocity cannot define one's relationship to everyone with whom one is in contact – unless one lives in a relatively small and self-contained community, such as a village or college, and spends most of one's time interacting with known people – the only possible glue for broader society is the trust that constructive and collaborative behaviour will, in the main, be reciprocated, even by strangers.

Virtual reciprocity is exhibited naturally by small actions, such as tipping in a restaurant you'll never visit again, by 'random acts of kindness', or by picking up litter. Virtual reciprocity can also be created by self-regulated person-to-person communities such as the auction site eBay, where individuals who sell goods are rated by their buyers and the results posted for everyone to see. Vendors guard their reputation as jealously as in a small village, at last giving some substance to the phrase 'global village'. Virtual reciprocity is strengthened by even a vague sense of commitment to liberal values and the society where one lives.

Third, there is locality and localization. As national identities slowly lose their force and cosmopolitan influences advance, local identity becomes vital to anchor the individual. Adherence to local identity – whether of a region, a town or a local sports team – is becoming stronger and stronger. Most of the dangers inherent in the trend to personalization can be neutralized by a trend to local community.

Reciprocity works best at the local level, where dense networks of personal obligation and identity can be most easily constructed and reinforced. This is why there tends to be less crime, less depression, less suicide and less alienation in smaller towns than in larger ones, in smaller countries than in larger ones, and in places with vibrant local communities. This is why we believe that democratic institutions and decisions should increasingly be devolved to local levels.

Finally, individualism and personalization are *moral* and *social* processes – something quite different from the common perception that individualization is amoral, immoral, asocial or anti-social. The popular perception derives from the very recent form of individualism that, at the risk of caricature, could be called 'Reaganite' or 'Thatcherite'. In the much longer historical perspective we have taken in this chapter, it's clear that neo-conservative individualism is at best a bastardization and at worst a travesty of genuine individualism – which is nothing less than humanity's quest for personal freedom and responsible self-expression.

Individualism originated in personal responsibility before God and has evolved into the belief that ethical authority comes from within, from the sacred self. Historically, individualism has always led to *higher* demands on the person, culminating in the modern Western assumption that everyone has a unique destiny to fulfil.

Individualism means *self-rule*, striving, trying to achieve the not-yet-achieved – not the absence of effort, ethics or care. Individualism makes life more fulfilling, yet also harder.

Individualism has always also been associated with *social* activity of like-minded people – whether it be the original Jesus movement; the guilds of free craftsmen and artisans; the self-government of burghers in their city states; the churches and sects springing from the Reformation; the glittering world of the Renaissance, with its schools of creative artists; the modern democratic and revolutionary movements; voluntary associations of workers; campus radicals; academic specialists; musical groups of all kinds; or the clusters of engineers and entrepreneurs in Silicon Valley.

Individualists can only express themselves by reaching out to other individualists, through talk and writing, professional association, and *being there*, in the place that most stimulates their creative juices. Inspired people have always gravitated toward the cities and regions populated by the same *genus* of individualists, and they still do. The Internet creates useful virtual communities but any creative person will tell you that it is no substitute whatever for the intensity of face-to-face contact between fellow enthusiasts.

Creative achievement of all types is incredibly localized. For example, the great majority of technological innovation in the world between 1880 and 1914 took place in just three cities – Berlin, New York and Boston. Since 1970, a similarly local pattern of high technology achievement has emerged, based in California and Seattle, Munich, Paris-Sud, the English M4 corridor, Cambridge and Oxford, and Tokyo-Yokahama. Sociological studies have explained Silicon Valley's extraordinary success as a function of its rich and complex social structure, where engineers, academics, venture capitalists and headhunters rub shoulders daily, gathering to swap ideas and gossip at their gyms and watering holes. The Valley is a magnet for bright young technological talent from everywhere around the world.

True individualists do not subvert local communities. They build them.

Conclusion

Individualism has always been the West's most strikingly original characteristic. As time has passed, the West's degree of individualism has progressively increased, culminating in today's *personalized society*, where individuals are not constrained or protected by hierarchy, but are autonomous and must rule themselves.

Individualism has been, and remains more than ever, crucial to the West's success. It lies behind the West's ethical values, optimism, science, political stability and economic growth.

Individualism is the quality most difficult for non-Western civilizations to imitate or import. Even dynamic countries, including many in Asia, which have successfully imported optimism, science, economic growth, and, to a degree, liberalism, have not become individualistic to anything like the extent of *every* Western country. Westerners, through their history and culture, are totally impregnated with individualism. Non-Westerners are not. This huge difference is unlikely to change fast, if at all.

The personalized society does erode the traditional, handed-down sense of community, and it does load stress onto individuals.

Nonetheless, the dangers of individualism are greatly exaggerated. In the shift from hierarchical society to personalized society, individualists can and do build personal reciprocity and local community. Individualists create far more than they destroy. Individualism has always been, and still is, ethically exacting and gregarious. The danger to Western civilization is not too much individualism, but too little. If the end of hierarchy results in the victim mentality and cynicism about personal achievement, the West is finished; it will no longer be the West.

The basic character of Europeans and Americans is unlimited personal striving and aspiration. Westerners invented personal responsibility, the concept of the self, personality and the obligation of self-differentiation. They are world-improvers and self-improvers, driven by passion and relentless energy. Individuals and individuality are at the heart of the idea of the West, at the heart of its flaws, and at the heart of all its matchless achievements. For the West, there may be no choice between extreme individuality and any other way of life. If the West's supremely demanding and unique brand of individualism ever falters, there will be nothing uniquely worthwhile left.

*   *   *

We have now finished our review of the six reasons why the West is different, why it has been so successful, and why the continuation of that success cannot be taken for granted. Where does this leave the relations between Westerners and non-Westerners? That's the issue we grapple with next, before finally answering our most vital question: Is the West set to trigger its own downfall?

8   The West and the Rest

What is the relationship between the West and the Rest? What beliefs drive 'Western foreign policy'? And will those beliefs advance or endanger Western civilization?

Every Western policymaker, and every citizen who thinks at all about the relationship between the West and the rest of the world, tends to operate, implicitly or explicitly, with one of six 'mental models':

1. *Western universalism*, the view that the West represents modernity and that all important areas of the world will naturally turn, sooner or later, to Western-style liberalism and capitalism.
2. *Liberal imperialism*, that is, the belief that the West should advance democracy and capitalism throughout the world, if necessary by force.
3. The approach we call *World-America*, which holds that the world will be happiest and safest if America and her allies impose universal peace and common economic policies, without worrying too much about democratic trappings.
4. *Fortress West*, where the West retreats into itself to protect its civilization, and effectively 'gives up' on the rest of the world.
5. The *cosmopolitan* view that the West and the Rest will eventually converge naturally toward common values and institutions.
6. The *coexistence and attraction* strategy, which has four prongs: respecting the diversity of other civilizations; being willing to coexist with them; reinvigorating Western ideals; and attracting the Rest to the West.

We will describe each strategy, lay bare its assumptions about the West and the Rest, and examine its track record and likely impact on Western civilization and the world.

Western universalism

In 1985, the distinguished British historian J. M. Roberts concluded a study of the West with these words:

> What seems clear is that the story of Western civilization is now the story of mankind, its influence so diffused that old oppositions and antitheses are now meaningless. 'The West' is hardly now a meaningful term, except to historians.[1]

Four years later, political scientist Francis Fukuyama went even further:

> We may be witnessing . . . the end of history as such: that is, the end of mankind's ideological evolution and the universalization of Western liberal democracy as the final form of human government.[2]

The assumptions underlying this approach are clear:

- The West was historically different from the Rest, but the Rest is becoming so similar to the West as to make 'the West' an obsolete expression.
- The virtues of the Western approach are so self-evident that everyone will come to adopt them.
- The 'Westernization' of the world will happen naturally without the West having to do anything much.

---

1   Roberts (2001).
2   Francis Fukuyama, 'The End of History?', *The National Interest*, 16 (Summer 1989), pp. 4, 18.

Although some citizens of the West may still believe this story, few policymakers do. We could invert J. M. Roberts' comment and say that the idea of Western universalism is now so discredited that it is of interest only to historians. Anyone who looks beyond the West's boundaries knows that many cultures around the world – not just militant Islam – are extremely resistant to Westernization. That serious social scientists in the 1980s and early 1990s could have imagined otherwise now seems an extraordinary manifestation of Western arrogance and triumphalism. We hope that our account has explained *why* the West is different from the Rest, that 2,000 years of unique historical accidents have shaped Western attitudes and made them so different from those held by people in earlier times and by people in most other civilizations today. The notion that the rest of the world will fall willingly into line with Western systems is simply fanciful.

Liberal imperialism

We examined *liberal imperialism* in Chapter 6. The aim of liberal imperialism is to make the world – or as much of it as possible – Western, by force if necessary. Democracy and capitalism are encouraged everywhere. When there is a plausible justification for invasion of recalcitrant countries, they are to be occupied until democracy and capitalism are secure.

Many Westerners share these assumptions:

- The West is different from the Rest.
- The West is superior in important respects to most of the Rest.
- The West is justified in imposing its civilization on the Rest, to make the world a better and more peaceful place, or simply to protect the West from extreme regimes.
- Given a long enough time horizon and the right policies, liberal imperialism can work.

There are three issues with liberal imperialism. First, is it is consistent with Western values? Second, is it practical? Third, can it succeed?

Is liberal imperialism liberal? Certainly, there is the commitment to introduce democracy and liberal institutions. But, as Russia and Iran demonstrate, it is possible to have tolerably free elections without having a liberal society. There is no doubt that capitalism can successfully be imposed from above. It is possible to create prosperity without spontaneous and principled action by large numbers of individuals. But not a liberal society. Western-style civilization or liberty cannot be reproduced except through the actions of many active, competent and confident individuals, motivated and driven on by the nature of their beliefs. The most valuable parts of Western civilization – the parts that are conspicuous today in their absence, as in Russia, Pakistan, Nigeria, Zimbabwe or Iraq – do not relate to wealth or formal democracy, but to individuals' sense of their own value and responsibility. Such civilization cannot be imposed. It can only bubble up from below, based on confidence, trust and deep personal belief in equality, initiative and responsibility.

Liberal imperialism does not lead to liberty. Imperialism may instead make the emergence of a liberal society slower, more difficult and less likely. Liberal society is most likely to emerge when countries are left alone to find their own salvation, through struggle and mutual cooperation. South Africa is instructive here. In 1990, very few people predicted the emergence of a liberal society. Yet it arrived, because of the actions of *South Africans*. Of course, even in apartheid's darkest days, many elements of Western civilization, represented by dissident politicians, journalists, authors and business leaders, managed to survive. What is impressive, however, is how South Africans made the transition not just to democracy but also to reconciliation and a liberal society. They did it the only way that can possibly stick – by taking responsibility for their own country, their past and their future.

Not only will liberal imperialism defeat the cause of liberty in places where it is imposed; it will also tend to subvert liberty in its home base. Liberal imperialism requires America's gigantic military muscle to be deployed in hostile terrain. Three results are inevitable, and are already beginning to happen. First, war will tend to coarsen and debase liberal ideals, within the US military, within US administrations, and in the country as a whole, as civil rights take second place to homeland security. (The same phenomenon may be observed to a lesser degree in contemporary Britain.) Second, America, traditionally the 'home of the free' and the natural friend and ally of people struggling for freedom everywhere around the globe, will become less and less popular. Third, the number of anti-American terrorists and the degree of their hatred of America will multiply. As terrorism increases, measures to deal with terrorism tend to become more and more illiberal. The vicious cycle is renewed and intensified.

The second issue is that imperialism requires imperialists. Although there are American and even British intellectuals, and a few American policymakers, who favour the extension of the American empire throughout the world, no empire in the world has ever changed the hearts and minds of its subject peoples without taking tens and usually hundreds of years to do so, nor without whole cadres of resident imperialists dedicated to inculcating their civilization within the people they ruled. Installing a puppet regime is easy. Robust local democracy cannot be imposed or installed; it has to grow naturally, encouraged by example and by expatriates who genuinely believe in it. Where are these American expatriates, willing to serve for decades away from home to advance democracy in Africa, the Middle East or Asia? They do not exist, at least not in sufficient numbers, with the long-haul dedication required.

The final problem with liberal imperialism is that there is no market for it. Even if the supply of imperialists existed, a willing response from local people would be required. That is pure fantasy. Imperialism is an idea whose time has gone. Even in the nineteenth and early twentieth centuries, when there were tens of thousands of dedicated British and other European imperialists, imperialism notched up far more failures than successes. Despite all the force and all the financial incentives in the world, European culture, in nearly every case, did not *take* with enough local people to make it self-sustaining after Europeans withdrew. As we have moved further and further into a world where the weaknesses of Western culture are apparent, and where the motives of Western empire builders are increasingly distrusted, it should be obvious to anyone with an ounce of common sense that peoples outside the West are not going to allow Western mores to be imposed on them.

George Orwell said that some ideas are so stupid that only intellectuals can believe in them. Communism was one example, and liberal imperialism is another. People outside the West will select what they want from the West that is compatible with their pre-existing beliefs and that serves their aspirations, discarding the remainder. Any organized attempt to impose the Western way of life *en bloc* is doomed not just to failure, but to retard the sensible and partial adoption of some elements of Western thinking by people with minds and cultures of their own.

World-America

Since 1918, and to a greater extent since 1945, but more particularly since 2001, there has been increasing support in American policy circles for the view that world peace and prosperity requires active international leadership and intervention by the United States. This doctrine, which we call *World-America*, is effectively imperialism shorn of burdensome democratic trappings.

It is not without its ideals, and not wholly designed to advance American interests. It recognizes the overwhelming military dominance of the United States, which is stronger than the next 17 nations put together. It sees the need for that power to be used responsibly to maintain good order and decency across the world.

Sometimes it is used in a way commanding general admiration

– as for example in the intervention to save the Bosnian people from genocide. But the World-America view goes way beyond humanitarian interventions.

The panoply of American-sponsored international organizations, from the World Bank to GATT to the IMF to the dozens of other international acronym bureaucracies, envisages a universal world economic, political and humanitarian order that follows broadly American patterns. The message is simple; there is one universal, modern way of conducting business and geopolitics, and it is the Western way: rational, market-based and global, allowing no boundaries to limit its sphere of influence.

World-America makes the following implicit judgements:

- The West represents modernity and is superior to the Rest.
- There should be a universal world formula based on the Western and particularly American pattern.
- The West should make the Rest conform to this pattern.
- The countries of the West should reduce their cultural and political diversity and conform to this pattern, if necessary sacrificing domestic interests in order to coincide with a universal world template.
- The template is recognizably American, but requires the United States to give up the option of reverting to narrow nationalism or isolationism. Crudely, World-America will become and remain the world's chief cop. Within the constraint of market forces, World-America will heavily influence the world's economic parameters (for example, money supply, interest rates, exchange rates and trade rules).

World-America has not yet fully arrived, nor is its advent inevitable or even probable. It is an open question. Leave aside the possibility that America may decline over the next century relative to other powers. There are also powerful forces within America itself championing 'national' America against 'cosmopolitan' and 'imperialist' elites, and influential populist forces in both political parties.

In 2004, Samuel Huntington concluded a book about America's identity with stirring words:

> Significant elements of American elites are favorably disposed to America becoming a cosmopolitan society. Other elites wish it to assume an imperial role. The overwhelming bulk of the American people are committed to a national alternative and to preserving and strengthening the American identity that has existed for centuries. America becomes the world. The world becomes America. America remains America. Cosmopolitan? Imperial? National? The choices Americans make will shape their future as a nation and the future of the world.[3]

Huntington notes that the American public is more nationalistic and less disposed to 'transnationalism' than its political and business leaders:

> . . . in six polls from 1978 to 1998, 96 to 98 per cent of the foreign policy elites favored the US taking an active part in world affairs, but only 59 to 65 per cent of the public did . . . the public has been much more reluctant than the leaders to use US military force to defend other countries.

Huntington, then, is against what we call World-America – and no doubt he speaks for many, and perhaps a majority, of ordinary Americans.[4] It is also clear that both Europe's political leaders and

---

3   Huntington (2004).
4   Polls suggest that, in ordinary times, the American public does not like foreign wars. It is only when these are relatively costless, or when there is a strong sense that America itself is threatened by external enemies, that Americans tend to favour war, and hence an American imperial role. The US Presidential Election of 2004 produced a tiny popular majority in favour of the incumbent President, who argued, against the balance of informed opinion, that 9/11 required war in Iraq. In the absence of terrorist outrages, that is, in normal circumstances, it is unlikely although not impossible that the American public would favour the World-American approach. American participation in overseas wars has always been 'sold' to a reluctant American public by its political elites rather than arising from a strong populist nationalism.

its peoples lean strongly against the World-American option by large majorities. But that does not mean it couldn't happen. The military and organizational infrastructure of World-America is already in place. We do not merely mean the 'alphabet soup' of international bureaucracies and other American-sponsored 'supra-national' agencies, of which the IMF (International Monetary Fund) is merely the most visibly effective World-American operator.[5] We also mean America's quite overwhelming military strength and presence. As Niall Ferguson says:

> Before the deployment of troops for the invasion of Iraq, the United States military had around 752 military installations in more than 130 countries. Significant numbers of American troops were stationed in 65 of these . . . If military power is the *sine qua non* of an empire, then it is hard to imagine how anyone could deny the imperial character of the United States today.[6]

America has the platform and power for the World-American role. It is easy to see how a fully-fledged World-America could arise. Imagine that American economic and cultural influences continue to spread widely. That universal free trade – inevitably favouring the strong – is imposed throughout the world. That American fundamentalism becomes even more influential, by forming a political bloc to back the most fundamentalist Presidential candidate; and also that fundamentalists become markedly more intolerant. There are renewed bomb attacks on US cities. Anti-terrorist measures increasingly constrain civil liberties. The power of the Presidency and its agencies goes up and up. Non-white immigration is halted. Crime is largely extirpated, by the

---

5 In saying the IMF is effective, we do not mean to impugn its incompetence. There are many cases where objective observers have examined the effects of IMF 'advice' to Third World countries, and found them wanting. The IMF is effective in ordering sovereign states around, not in making their economies successful.

6 Ferguson (2004).

simple device of locking up anyone who is a criminal, or might become one. *Pax Americana* is imposed throughout the globe. Pro-American puppet regimes are installed in many Middle Eastern and Asian countries, and prove much more durable than when the West felt obliged to try to introduce democracy. Nonetheless, disaffected youths swell the ranks of anti-American terrorists.

With military, scientific and economic supremacy, World-America comprises a new and enduring civilization. As ruthless as imperial Rome, World-America might rule most of the world, or perhaps all of it, alongside allies in Europe, Japan and Korea. Powers such as China, Russia and India pose major problems; but after a few years or decades of bloody conflict, peace, docility and prosperity span the globe. Implausible as it might seem today, World-America might even confound its critics and save the planet by authoritarian imposition of highly rigorous and world-universal 'green' practices, winning the plaudits of serious environmentalists everywhere. The streets of all the world's cities would be safe for tourists of whatever hue. The only casualties would be liberty, and many venerable civilizations around the world, including the Western one.

Fortress West

The fourth 'mental model' of the West and the Rest is rarely artic-ulated openly. It is often implicit and sometimes explicit in the rhetoric and policies of American populists and isolationists, and nationalists and xenophobes in several European countries. These 'fringe' politicians are more significant than they appear – they often say what is left unsaid in polite circles but thought by many, including some mainstream lawmakers and the 'illiberal third' said to lurk within most electorates. Fortress West implies 'Damn the Rest':

- The West is superior to the Rest.
- The Rest mean trouble for the West.
- Isolate the Rest from the West.

The West is lambasted by 'anti-globalization' protesters for exploiting the Third World. Fortress West politicians turn this protest on its head, correctly noting that every Western country does most of its trade with other developed countries, so the need for integration with the Third World is much less than commonly thought. Although Fortress West is right-wing, it is very different from World-America's universal imperialism.

The Fortress West scenario is simple and plausible. Under renewed terrorist assault and the growth in immigrant populations, the West retreats into itself to protect its civilization. As with World-America, immigration into the West is virtually stopped. To avoid conflict with the rest of the world, all attempts to spread democracy and capitalism are abandoned. The West stops trying to extend trade beyond its boundaries. Technological diffusion is discouraged. There is fearsome defence of the West's territory. Military adventures are eschewed. In erecting its fortress and, in effect, giving up on the rest of the world, the architects of Fortress West hope that growth in the rest of the world's population and economies will founder, mitigating ecological danger.

The strategy might not work. For a start, there would be a continuing need to engage with the rest of the world for raw materials and resources. Moreover, as with highly protected, 'gated' communities in turbulent places, we would probably see growing fear, insecurity and paranoia within, and swelling frustration, envy and anger outside.

Cosmopolitan

The cosmopolitan view, like Western universalism, holds that the world will sooner or later end up with one dominant and almost exclusive modern civilization. Unlike Western universalists, however, cosmopolitans hold the more pleasing and balanced notion that the world's cultures will intermingle and interpenetrate each other. Eventually East and West *will* meet, and the world will be one big family:

- The East is becoming more like the West, and the other way round.
- Human aspirations are universal, and cultural differences are but mild obstacles on the path to universal modernity and mores.
- There are advantages to both Western and Eastern ways of approaching issues, and eventually the market will clear in favour of the ways that most conduce toward human happiness.
- Given cultural convergence, there is no need for any particular Western strategy towards the Rest (or the other way round).

Although they might not assent fully to these propositions, most urbane and civilized Westerners have been profoundly affected by the cosmopolitan view. Richard E. Nisbett, in his book *The Geography of Thought*, shows how Eastern and Western ways of thinking are different, but suggests that there are some signs of convergence.

There has never been greater interest among Westerners in Eastern philosophy and cross-fertilization of ideas, from Zen Buddhism to the Mind, Body, Spirit movement, from Gandhi's non-violent passive resistance to the tactics of Martin Luther King, from Marxism to Maoism. Concepts such as 'karma' have penetrated the vocabulary of millions in the West, while Western concepts of capitalism have been profoundly modified in places such as Japan and China to marry the power of the market to more hierarchical and communitarian societies. One of the most important Western scientific innovations since 1970, the inter-disciplinary study of 'chaos' and 'complexity', can be viewed as the outcome of 'Eastern' holistic thinking, showing how complex systems emerge and adapt, creating something bigger and different than their constituent parts.[7]

On a less exalted but perhaps more influential level, different cultures have happily imitated – or at least caricatured – each other's cuisine. The West has imported Asian and eclectic so-called 'world' (that is, non-Western) food, in return for the relentless export of hamburgers, pizza, branded soft drinks and assembly line fried chicken segments. No doubt all the cross-continental exchanges of people, products and propositions are doing something to broaden the mind as well as the bottom, helping to make the world a more tolerant as well as a less variegated place.

Yet there is something rather superficial about the cosmopolitan thesis. There is no evidence that the gulf between Western and non-Western ways of thinking is becoming smaller, even in fully developed capitalist economies such as Japan. Consumerism, Hollywood, Western brands and popular music are making great strides outside the West, but the appeal is so great precisely because it is skin deep, a quick fix of modernity requiring no adjustment of fundamental attitudes to life and society and no need to act differently.

The importation of Eastern ideas, and in particular religions, into the West is, in the main, equally superficial, a light coating of easily acquired spirituality, a travesty of true Eastern religion. The Western taste for exotic aesthetic and religious experience is not new, dating at least from the middle of the nineteenth century. Nor has it changed Western attitudes one whit – the ever greater

---

7   See Richard Koch (2001) *The Natural Laws of Business*, Doubleday, New York, chapter 10; James Gleick (1987) *Chaos*, Little, Brown, New York; M. Mitchell Waldrop (1992) *Complexity*, Simon & Schuster, New York.

interest in Buddhist and other Eastern religions which exemplify quiet reflection and awareness of the world beyond oneself has coincided with ever greater Western individualism and constant acceleration in the pace of life. The words of Oswald Spengler from 1918 resonate today:

> . . . we have in the European–American world of today the occultist and thesopist fraud, the American Christian Science, the untrue Buddhism of drawing-rooms, the religious arts-and-crafts business (brisker in Germany than even in England) that caters for groups and cults of Gothic or late-Classical or Taoist sentiment. Everywhere it is just a toying with myths that no one really believes, a tasting of cults that it is hoped might fill the inner void. Materialism is shallow and honest, mock-religion shallow and dishonest.[8]

The cosmopolitan theory utterly fails to understand the wrenching impact of Western civilization on most non-Western societies. Since around 1850, the latter have found it increasingly difficult to ignore the West and its ideas and practices, not least because of the prosperity and advances in life expectancy that they offer. Yet it has proved, for most non-Westerners, difficult or impossible to become truly Western, just as it was impossible even for Lawrence of Arabia truly to become an Arab. To many people outside the West, there is still something alien, even abhorrent, about Western culture and individualism.

The cosmopolitans like to imply that intellectual trade between the West and the Rest is two-way, essentially an equal exchange of Western and non-Western innovations. But this is simply not the case. Peter Watson, a scrupulously fair observer, recently wrote a history of ideas in the twentieth century. 'When the work was conceived,' he tells us, 'it was my intention to make the text as

---

8   Spengler (1991), p. 346.

international and multicultural as possible.' This proved more difficult than he had expected:

> I began to work my way through scholars who specialised in the major non-Western cultures: China, Japan, southern and central Africa, the Arab world. I was shocked (that is not too strong a word) to find that they all (I am not exaggerating, there were no exceptions) came up with the same answer, that in the twentieth century, the non-Western cultures have produced no body of work that can compare with the West . . . a good proportion of these scholars were themselves . . . non-Western . . . More than one made the point that the chief intellectual effort of his or her own (non-Western) culture in the twentieth century has been a coming to terms with modernity, learning how to cope with or respond to Western ways and Western patterns of thought, chiefly democracy and science . . .
>
> Of course, there are important Chinese writers and painters of the twentieth century, and we can all think of important Japanese film directors, Indian novelists, and African dramatists . . . But, it was repeatedly put to me, there is no twentieth-century Chinese equivalent of, say, surrealism or psychoanalysis, no Indian contribution to match logical positivism, no African equivalent of the *Annales* school of history. Whatever list you care to make of twentieth-century innovations, be it plastic, antibiotics and the atom or stream-of-consciousness novels, *vers libre* or abstract expressionism, it is almost wholly Western.[9]

The cosmopolitan view is desperately naïve. Patterns of thought and action are deeply rooted in the history, geography, religion and power structures of particular societies, and cannot be swapped at will through consumerism, cultural exchanges or wishful thinking.

---

9 Watson (2000).

Coexistence and attraction

The option we think adapts best to cultural realities is our own synthesis, the coexistence and attraction strategy. It observes:

- There are several different non-Western civilizations, all substantially different from Western civilization;
- According to the criteria that Westerners hold dear, Western civilization is a stunning triumph. It has been more successful than any other civilization at increasing its citizens' welfare, lifespan, dignity, creativity and individual freedom, and, in the past half-century, prospects for Westerners of a life free from the ravages of war.
- The downside to Western civilization is its relentless disruption of tradition, established thought patterns, religious and secular authority, personal and social stability, and the planet's ecology.
- The West has intruded on other civilizations massively, by force, by economic expansion, and through its unprecedented powers of communication. No other civilization has intruded on the West in a comparable way for at least 500 years.
- The West offers huge benefits and huge costs to non-Westerners. The benefits are mainly in the form of personal opportunity and freedom. The costs are mainly social disruption, personal confusion and challenge to established beliefs and identities.
- Though no non-Western civilization rates the benefits of the West as highly as Westerners, and all non-Western civilizations rate the costs brought by the West more heavily than Westerners do, different non-Western civilizations, and different people and groups within them, weigh the benefits and costs of Westernization differently. Civilizations fall into three main categories:
  - Those at least somewhat receptive to Western civilization, because of historical exposure to it and because of cultural and/or ethnic commonalities (Latin American, Russian/ Orthodox, some African).
  - Those that appreciate Western science and growth and are

open to Western know-how, but want to preserve their own culture and values (Japanese, Chinese, Buddhist, probably Hindu, some African).

– Those substantially or implacably opposed to Western civilization (some Islamic).

• In every civilization there is a minority (sometimes a very small minority) of ambitious individuals who identify with Western values. These individuals are likely to seek to emigrate to the West. This process, at least for a time, siphons off the most pro-Western non-Westerners and makes non-Western societies less pro-Western.

We believe that all these points are substantiated by the evidence we have presented, or are reasonable inferences from it. If this is accepted, what might the West do in relation to the Rest to advance its interests and security? We think three things.

First, *respect diversity*. The world is not going to become Western. Neither the West, nor the Rest, is going to become the world. Diversity is here to stay. If mutual understanding is to prevail, Westerners need to be respectful, and stop assuming that non-Westerners have or should have the same values. The most the West can expect from certain civilizations is that they tolerate Western ways, even when they abhor them. We cannot expect such tolerance unless we too tolerate what we abhor.

Second, *reinvigorate Western ideals*. In the contest of ideas and ideals, numbers do not count. If they did, views and knowledge would never change. What matters is, to some extent, the intrinsic value of the ideas and ideals,[10] and to a larger extent the intensity with which they are believed. Every dominant religion started as a tiny sect, able to convert through the power of example and

---

10 In talking of the 'intrinsic value' of ideas, we do not mean to imply that some ideas are absolutely true or valuable, only that some ideas are better than others at fulfilling particular human objectives in a specific environment at a specific time.

persuasion. The ideological leadership of the West – the fact that no other civilization has such an advanced or coherent set of ideas that works so well – is no guarantee that the ideology will remain dominant or even extant. If we respect diversity, and do not impose our ideals by force, then intensity of belief is paramount.

Belief is not mainly a matter of *instrumental* belief, that an idea is worthwhile because it is materially useful. Belief is mainly a matter of *ethical* and/or *spiritual* belief, that an idea is also an ideal, a worthy human aspiration. The West can sell oceans of Coca-Cola, but oceans of Coca-Cola cannot sell the West. What the West can uniquely offer is not affluence, because this can come, as Japan has shown, without adopting the full set of Western values. What the West has to offer is personal freedom. If Westerners do not value personal freedom much, or affect not to, the West will have nothing to give, and nothing that will be preserved.

Third, *attract the Rest to the West.* Nowadays, one does not gain a spouse or romantic partner by force, or by importunate and over-the-top wooing. One attracts by being friendly, engaging, pleasing, intriguing, even diffident or coy – in short, by *being attractive.* In the modern market for partners and friends, a relationship is sought, not sold. If there is any selling, it is extremely soft and subtle.

So it is with civilizations and societies. In the nineteenth century, the West extended its civilization by force. In just 20 years, between 1875 and 1895, six European Powers grabbed over a quarter of the globe's land and integrated those countries into their empires. The twentieth century saw the collapse of Western empires – in purely geographical terms, in territory and number of subjects, the West did indeed decline, as Spengler foretold in 1918, and to a small fraction of its former bloated size. In truth, this was no decline: it was simply the unwinding of an unsustainable project, the forced conversion of alien cultures and peoples.

A sea change occurred in the middle of the twentieth century, one of those life-enhancing shifts in attitude and behaviour that are often under-celebrated or barely noted. In the West, the idea of seizing territory, of invading a neighbouring or distant country and claiming its land and people as one's own, suddenly went out of fashion, perhaps for ever. The benefit in terms of human happiness and absence of misery is massive and incalculable.

The contemporary way to spread influence and ideas is voluntarily. Not by force, but by attraction. That is why Western ideas – especially Christianity, optimism, growth, science and liberalism – have steadily made greater inroads in non-Western societies since 1950 than they ever did in the nineteenth century. In the last 60 years, the West has been more successful in advancing its best ideas where it has eschewed using force (Eastern Europe, Russia, most of South America, South Africa, parts of Asia) than where it has used a heavy hand (Korea, Vietnam, the Middle East). Not only does force have a huge cost in lives and suffering; it also does not work very well in attaining its objectives. Blood and missiles do not win hearts and minds. Force has higher costs and fewer benefits than attraction. It seems this lesson has not been fully learned, even by the West, but with a long enough historical sweep it is obvious and incontrovertible.

Communism, at least in its fully developed and full-blooded state-driven forms, was one of the great evils of the twentieth century and indeed of all time – Stalin and Mao were even more prolific in their murders than Hitler. Did nuclear weapons end communism? Did Star Wars? Did force of arms? Certainly, without the counterbalancing strength of NATO, Stalin and Mao would have enslaved even more lands and peoples. But if we ask which was more important in ending communism, hard power or soft power, force or attraction, the answer is clear. Consider what would have happened in the Soviet empire between 1980 and 1991 if its rulers, and in particular Mikhail Gorbachev, had not been seduced by Western values. They would have suppressed the revolts in Eastern Europe with Stalinist ferocity. They had the troops, but not the will. The Soviet Union dismantled itself because it had ceased to believe in its own anti-Western values. Soon after, more adroitly, if less completely, the Chinese empire moved in a similar direction.

The sequence is evident. Ideas gain ground when they are fresh and believed in passionately. More people come to believe them intensely. Their power changes the world. Then the ideas lose their energizing force. They become mature, unexciting, conventional, formal, the object of lip service. Cynicism and self-interest abound. Novel ideas are sexier, more appealing. The cycle begins again. In the battle of ideas, you have to believe before you can persuade. You have to be attractive before you can attract. You can have the most wonderful story in the world, but if you do not believe it, nobody else will either. Where are the true believers today?

If the West believes in its values and wants to spread its influence – both because the West will be more secure and the world happier as a result – it must, wherever it possibly and creatively can, use soft power and not hard power, carrot not stick, example not direction, pull not push. It must stick to its values, not violate them. America's hugely lopsided military dominance is a menace, not merely to her enemies, but also to herself.

The process of attraction will not produce quick results. It is hard to see certain places – say China or the Islamic world – adopting liberal democracy or individualism. Even with oppressive regimes, the West's best policy is surely to let the attractiveness of the West influence their people. Peaceful contact with decent Westerners may slowly erode anti-Western prejudice and thus, eventually, the anti-Western character of those regimes. If the regimes remain firmly anti-Western, that will be because ultimately Western values do not prove attractive enough to non-Westerners. That would be disappointing. But, provided the regimes do not harbour terrorists, or invade Western territory, the West can live with such an outcome, and should do so with good grace.

Conclusion

The world is not going to become a melting pot. Nor will the world adopt Western values naturally. To try to force this outcome, or even advance it substantially by coercion, is illiberal, impractical and futile. Certainly, America could ruthlessly impose its empire on much, or possibly all, of the world, but liberty and the attractive parts of Western civilization would fall by the wayside. The same result would follow any serious attempt of the West to retreat into its own *laager*.

The only realistic and sensible alternative is for the West to respect cultural differences, exercise patience and forbearance, believe in its best ideas, spread its influence by example, let the ideas and their results speak for themselves, and gradually disarm enemies and attract fellow travellers.

For sure, America, Europe and allies of the West must respond to any encroachment on their soil with immediate, effective and proportionate force. No powerful and self-confident civilization can be expected to do anything else. But ultimately the peace, security and happiness of the West and the world depend on the imitation of America through most of its history, and Europe since 1945 – the avoidance of tyranny and aggression, the refusal to advance economic or political interests by invading and occupying foreign lands, and extending the hand of friendship and cooperation first to one's neighbours, and then to all who come in peace.

It is a tall order. There are always pretexts and rationales for backsliding into aggression – historically the natural instinct, the default option, of any powerful state or civilization. The West has often soaked itself and its enemies in blood. Has Western civilization evolved to the point where the cycle of mutual hatred can be broken? Do Westerners truly believe in liberty and compassion? Will Western foreign policy be based on the attraction strategy? Will America and Europe unite to put the best of their heritage forward, to realize the potential of their common civilization?

Or will the West snatch defeat from the jaws of victory? In the final chapter, we assess the odds.

9   Is Suicide Inevitable?

It's time to pull together the threads of our argument, and see if there is any way to reconcile the best of Western civilization with the powerful self-imposed trends that are tearing it apart. Our thesis may be boiled down to three simple points.

First, in the last two centuries, in its best manifestation, Western civilization attained something which no other civilization has ever managed: an immensely rich society and culture, rich not only in living standards, where each generation could expect to surpass the level reached by its parents, but rich in something infinitely more precious, rich in freedom.

Freedom, to an extent often overlooked, is materially derived – freedom from wild animals looking for their next meal; freedom from hunger; freedom from wind, rain, heat and cold; freedom from ignorance and disease; freedom from back-breaking labour; freedom from poverty of all kinds.

Freedom is also freedom from oppression by fellow humans – freedom from slavery; freedom from forced work; freedom from involuntary military service; freedom from robbers and violence; freedom from parents, bosses and government coercion; from discrimination on grounds of gender, race, nationality, background or sexual preference; freedom from anything which denies human dignity and rights to fair and equal treatment.

Finally, freedom is positive – the freedom to create one's own life; the freedom to learn about the world and to contribute to new learning; the freedom to vote and help determine who will govern; the freedom to choose one's own work, friends, religion and living arrangements; the freedom to make life better for oneself and one's circle.

By these standards, Western civilization is far from perfect. But it is so much better than any other civilization, past or present, as to deserve celebration and preservation. Despite all the threats to the ideals of Western civilization, it is closer today to those ideals than in 1900 or 1950.

Our second point is that Western civilization resulted from a long and slow process, based ultimately on distinctive beliefs about the world and the nature of humans, and on actions in accordance with those beliefs. This is true of any civilization, but it is particularly true of the West, because the West has placed more emphasis than any other civilization on the role of ordinary men and women, and on their spontaneous action to improve society.

Institutions are important, of course, in running society, but institutions are less fundamental than beliefs, at least in the West, because it is beliefs that determine and change institutions. Institutions are, in a sense, *frozen beliefs*, and institutions were, and are, often unfrozen and refrozen in the West in accordance with new beliefs. For example, new beliefs led to the Protestant Reformation, and to new churches. In the West, beliefs are always more important than institutions, because Westerners believe they have the right and responsibility to change institutions if the latter no longer fit with their beliefs. Beliefs lead to actions. Eventually the actions become second nature; the beliefs behind the actions may no longer be articulated or even appreciated. At this stage, when the belief is nearly or completely unconscious, it is at its strongest and most powerful.

A good example is the 'Protestant ethic', which led ordinary people to view their 'calling', their work, as the most important thing in their lives and as a form of self-expression. This serious view of the individual's responsibility arose from Calvinist and Lutheran doctrines, but within a century or two had essentially become automatic and detached from religion.

In defining what is different about the West, therefore, we have excavated the beliefs that determined, and determine, the characteristic distinguishing actions of Westerners. We have found six dominant beliefs and action patterns that have determined the Western character – Christianity, optimism, science, growth, liberalism and individualism. The six 'success factors' are now baked into characteristic and routine ways of thinking and acting that do not necessarily require reaffirmation or awareness of the original doctrines behind each belief. For instance, Westerners believe in 'one person, one vote' and would be very upset if the vote were taken away from them, but they do not need to know that the idea of democracy was given distinctive form by the seventeenth-century notion of the social contract. Another example: Westerners generally believe in the ideas of personal responsibility, self-improvement and compassion for those less well off. They do not need to be Christians to share these values, even though the ideas were derived from primitive Christianity.

Beliefs and action patterns that determine the nature of society arise only slowly and through shared experience. Our six ideas emerged in close collaboration with each other, over very long periods of time. Consider, for example, the relationship between growth, liberalism and individualism. Western free market, individualistic and democratic society took hundreds of years to surface and triumph. It came slowly, largely from below, from the spontaneous actions of European merchants, craftsmen and artisans who first created new wealth and then were able to bargain for their freedom. It required the gradual building of habits of cooperation between those in power and those rising in society, where each side had something to offer the other. It needed confidence and self-esteem from large numbers of individuals, each drawing on inner resources and concepts of human dignity, equality and responsibility for action. Economic progress preceded political progress. Economic progress required individual human initiative, which in turn required widespread *belief* in the worth and power of individuals, and in their ability to improve their lives and those of the community they served.

Our third and final point is that we are at that treacherous, fascinating stage, where the beliefs and actions underpinning a civilization are under attack, perhaps signalling a move from one civilization to another. When civilizations disappear, they either evolve into another civilization, or else collapse under the difficulty of adapting old ways to deal successfully with new circumstances – usually new climates, or more powerful enemies. We have seen that all six of the West's fundamental beliefs have come under vicious and sustained attack in the last century, *from within the West itself.* How far have the ideas been invalidated by new thinking or experience? Are new beliefs and new actions necessary to sustain the success of the West? Let us summarize our analysis, for each of the six key attributes.

Christianity

It is easy to become fascinated by the lively and often virulent controversies within the churches, between various religions and between believers and non-believers, yet fail to notice one simple fact – the arguments have not changed society's values or patterns of action. The Christian heritage – individual responsibility and development, self-improvement centred on love, and the commitment to equality and compassion – long ago burst the banks of organized religion. It would be a brave Christian or atheist who asserted that there was much difference in terms of personal responsibility, love and compassion between the typical Western Christian and non-believer.

The rise and rise of the self-help and self-improvement movement in the past two centuries is testimony that the spirit of Christianity has become widely diffused and deeply impregnated within Western society. Christian ideas made it possible for society to advance through the initiative of quite ordinary people. Christianity also made it possible to conceive of a common, united civilization beyond the range of individual tribes and nations, based on principles of fairness and equality. This conceptual breakthrough is the basis of modern, complex society, where conflict is largely domesticated and disarmed and there is spontaneous and willing cooperation between hundreds of millions of individuals. No non-Western civilization has ever enjoyed this mix of activism, based on individual responsibility and initiative, with non-coercive social harmony, except through the influence of the West itself.

We therefore give a green light for contemporary Western civilization on the issue of Christianity.

Optimism

The eclipse of optimism is a warning for Western civilization. Only confident and forward-looking civilizations march forward. For sure, optimism and pessimism are fashions; they come and go. There are always good reasons to be optimistic, and equally compelling reasons to be pessimistic. Yet, optimism is integral to Western success. If optimism does not return, to Europeans as well as Americans, the continued success of the West will be lopsided at best. On the grounds that optimism is a virtue, we award, in traffic-light terms, a flashing yellow light; but this may be too optimistic.

Science

Western science arose from a conviction that the universe was rational, created by a dependable and omnipotent God. It was possible to discover the secrets of the universe because it was predictable and internally consistent. Science had moral authority, not just because it improved the life of humankind, but also because it traced the glory of God.

In the last century, however, science has seemed to reveal a universe that is unpredictable, strange and morally blind, without any discernible purpose or rationale. It is no accident that the West has seen a rise of irrational and superstitious beliefs at the same time that science has lost its confidence that nature makes sense. Through no fault of its own, but simply through the process of discovery, Western science has forfeited the moral authority enjoyed by earlier and less informed scientists, the confidence that their work revealed a beautifully consistent and meaningful universe. Sadly, too, the removal of science's internal idealistic logic has coincided with a quite new awareness that science may not always be humanity's friend. Nuclear, chemical and biological weapons – unthinkable without the new scientific world-view – may cause collective world suicide. These weapons cannot be 'uninvented'; nobody knows how to control them. The decentralization of society, and of access to knowledge, was the twentieth century's most profound and enduring trend.

The failing authority of science is, we think, another yellow light. Why not red? Well, though often unpopular, Western science has never been more vibrant, more useful, better attuned to the business community, better funded (at least in America), or closer to understanding the nature of our universe. Scientists are self-confident. Open innovation is triumphing. What ordinary citizens think about science matters, yet the prospect of an anti-scientific or post-scientific West is remote.

Growth

Economic growth is secure, all too secure. The remorseless advance of machine-based industry has profoundly disturbed the earth's ecological balance. Against that, optimists may argue that the West is generating a new, 'green' source of 'weightless' growth that uses fewer finite resources, substituting the infinite resource of human imagination. But it will take many decades to transfer the new 'personalized economy' fully to non-Western countries, and it can only be done at all in the unlikely event that they come to embrace Western patterns of thought and action.

Meanwhile, non-Western countries are catching up with the

West's old levels of industrial production and consumption. If developing countries eventually reached current levels of developed country consumption, the negative effects on the planet, as we have seen, would be increased 12 times. Even if we somehow contrived to avoid planetary collapse, our lands would no longer be green and pleasant.

If there is to be a cataclysmic end to Western civilization – rather than the evolution of that civilization into a different new civilization – ecological suicide is by far the most likely cause. Another yellow light – flashing strongly.

Individualism

Individualism has become so integral to Western culture, above all in the past half-century, that the demise of individualism is highly improbable. Western civilization, and no other, has evolved the *personalized economy* and the *personalized society*, where individuals are stand-alone entities, autonomous, self-creating or self-destroying, free from authority and not insulated against personal failure. For Westerners, the triumph of individualism has brought immense benefits, in stimulating creativity, enlarging every dimension of opportunity and freedom, almost creating a new species of humanity, *homo autonomous*.

Individualism has also corroded community, and greatly heightened personal anxiety.

Western individualism is hated by foes of the West, and causes much angst within the West, particularly among intellectuals. Yet, we argue, the recent prominence of 'Reaganite' and 'Thatcherite' individualism has misled us all. The self-regarding, society-denying strain of individualism is *not* intrinsic to individualism, nor even a proper subset of it. Selfish individualism is a late-twentieth-century heresy, almost an oxymoron. Individualism arose because God required the individual, previously safe within the group, to stand before him and account for his or her actions. Individualism always advanced in tandem with Christian and liberal values; it has been a liberating, responsible and democratic force. The main expression of Western individualism, from the sixteenth century until at least the 1950s, has been the so-called Protestant ethic. The key thing about the Protestant ethic was not self-denial, nor even hard work, but rather the belief that the individual should achieve self-esteem and worldly success through making a significant contribution to economic activity. The definition of individualism, and success, was therefore highly *social*, even when it took the form of making as much money as possible. In practice, both individuals and Western societies advanced along the path of greater individualism at the same time that they gained greater liberty and discharged greater responsibilities to fellow citizens.

Individualism is, and always has been, ethically exacting. It is also highly gregarious – the greatest individualists, from Jesus Christ to Joan of Arc to today's artists and business magnates, have been strong communicators and community builders. Individualism loosens automatic social bonds, it is true, but it allows – even requires – new and self-chosen bonds to be created, as reciprocity replaces authority.

We conclude, therefore, that the problem for Western civilization is not individualism, but our partial failure to embrace it properly, maturely, socially and altruistically. Even so, there is no green light here. The enemies of individualism, and the genuine difficulties – psychological even more than economic – that individualism creates for the less successful members of society, dictate another flashing yellow light.

Liberalism

We have left liberalism to last, because it's here we detect the greatest vulnerability. We have observed five self-inflicted reverses for Western liberalism – misdirected anti-terrorism, the resurgence of so-called 'liberal' imperialism, the fragmentation and devaluation of democratic politics, the moral emptiness of modern liberalism, and ultra-liberal relativism, which says that there is nothing special about Western liberal society after all, and incubates the 'victim' mentality.

What is most alarming is the *structural* nature of liberalism's reverses. The health of liberalism is profoundly affected by the *decentralization, fragmentation, and atomization* sweeping the West. As Western societies mature, grow more complex and more prosperous, and as economies become more personalized, power and decision-making in society become more and more devolved, ultimately to the most active and creative individuals within it. These individuals, for the first time in history, do not comprise a class, an elite, or an 'establishment'. They have no common family or social ties, no common ideology, and no common loyalty. Unlike all their predecessors, *they do not need these attributes to be successful.* And so, by and large, they do not have the values and networks that used to sustain liberal society.

This narrowing of horizons (let us call it 'atomization') brings large benefits – it can greatly enlarge freedom – and yet it may be the force that ultimately destroys Western civilization. The irony is that atomization can only be reversed by an act of political will, most likely by a reversion to authoritarian rule. So it is tempting to reach the gloomy conclusion that if the West's civilization is not undone by atomization and decentralization, it will probably be undone by re-centralization.

Does the crisis of liberalism deserve a red or yellow light? We say it's the biggest issue facing the West, for two almost opposite reasons. Liberalism is deeply rooted in the West, it is almost unstoppable, and yet it provokes a vicious backlash from illiberal forces outside and within Western society. Individualism does not *really* divide the West, since even Westerners who claim to be anti-individualists are, by any other civilization's criteria, ardent individualists. But a large minority of Westerners, particularly in America, and among Christian fundamentalists, hates liberalism.

Simultaneously, anti-Western terrorists – who of course also hate liberalism, along with individualism – are so far having extraordinary and undeserved success in stoking the fires of Western neo-imperialism, yet another anti-liberal force. As with communism and fascism, the twin enemies of extreme Islamism and ultra-conservatism in America and Europe find common ground in trashing liberalism.

On top of all this, the *quality* and *depth* of Western liberalism is nearing an all-time low. Even more dangerous than anti-liberal sentiment in the West is the cynicism and apathy displayed by large segments of the Western population who used to be, demographically or in terms of lifestyle and attitudes, liberalism's greatest upholders – the upwardly mobile, intellectuals, libertarians, trades unionists, and what used to be called the working classes. These often disparate segments each used to provide large numbers of people with strongly liberal views, and now provide far fewer.

This sounds like a red light – but is it really?

*   *   *

In summing up our thesis, we come back time and again to the *common purpose* of members of society, which ultimately derives from deeply held and often quite submerged beliefs. In the past 400 years, the West has engaged in a grand experiment, progressively removing the constraints on the freedom and power of all society's members. Conservatives have always held that the experiment was risky – many said foolhardy – because it only takes a small minority of malcontents to ruin society. Criminals aside, however, the experiment has worked: by and large, there is far less restraint on individuals in the West than at any time in the past, and anywhere else in the world today, and yet Western society works amazingly well. Hundreds of millions of individuals go about their work and their lives and manage to cooperate effectively without even realizing the extent of their cooperation and how miraculous it is. This grand experiment could never have worked without the powerful influence of the West's six seminal ideas.

Now, what happens when trends in society – like atomization, like the ecological challenge, like the existence of terrifying weapons accessible to fanatics, like the huge asymmetrical military power of the United States today – weaken the ideas underpinning unconscious cooperation, either because the ideas have no answer to the new problems, or because ordinary people do not realize that their best hope of preserving their wonderful civilization is to use and adapt the ideas which have been so successful to date? Self-imposed problems go unresolved; or else the attempt to resolve the problems changes the nature of the civilization.

Approaches to a new Western civilization?

In the twentieth century there were two serious attempts, both arising within the West, to subvert the West's previous winning ideas and introduce a new 'civilization' – communism and Nazism. Both new systems crushed the essence of Christianity, liberalism and individualism, while adopting bastardized versions of optimism, science and growth. It is an interesting speculation whether Nazi or Soviet civilizations, being based on denials of human dignity, compassion, creativity and true empirical science, could ever have ruled the world and lasted. Maybe they could, if they had first wiped out the competition from Western civilization – this nearly happened in 1941. But the Nazis and Soviets shared the weaknesses as well as the strengths of highly iconoclastic extremism. It is easy to imagine a less extreme, more pragmatic civilization that might be highly successful, keep more of the Western heritage and yet jettison many core values of the West, to the point where it would represent a different civilization.

In the previous chapter, we examined three competing contemporary influential Western strategies: so-called liberal imperialism, World-America and Fortress West. All are plausible scenarios. If what comes to pass is any of the three strategies, or any admixture of them, the West will have abandoned its characteristic civilization and the vision of America's founding fathers. Their design was universal liberty. They wished the liberty that their country had struggled and suffered to attain to be extended to the ends of the earth, so that oppression and prejudice, dictatorships and war could be banished, as far as humanly possible, to the benighted past. Their dream inspired the most effective Western idealists of the last two centuries. Certainly, they were optimists whose reach exceeded their grasp. Yet they moved the world – always in their day, as ours, a turbulent place, beset with towering problems – significantly closer to their model.

Idealism is retreating. It is not just that liberalism is so weak and vapid that it is easily violated. The new realists, the cynics and the throng of 'victims', under-achievers, and the wilfully uneducated, are active or passive destroyers not just of liberal ideals, but of all ideals – of the spirit of Christianity, with its restless activism, conscience and injunctions to compassion; of the optimistic view of humanity, which looks more at the potential of men and women than at their flaws; of confidence in the value and moral importance of extending knowledge; of the possibility of using economic growth to eliminate hunger, indignity and want; and of responsible individualism.

All these beliefs are essential to the character and progress of the West. Actions motivated by these beliefs are integral to the rise of the West. These ideals have proved their practicality over centuries. They work. They inspire. They lead to greater results and greater cooperation than any other set of beliefs and actions has ever done. Every society that violated these ideals, or had them in poorer measure and inferior versions, has failed to work as well as the West; or, in many cases, failed to work at all. So when we lose these ideals, we should not be surprised if there are all kinds of unintended consequences. At the moment, we are harvesting our past heritage, living off and using up the goodwill and human spirit planted by our predecessors.

Can the Western vision be realized?

Civilizations move forward or they move back. They realize dreams
or they discard them. In the last 230 years, the West came tantaliz-
ing close to a completely new form of human experience, one
marked by very high ideals, including, within that common civilization, the abolition of poverty, the relief of suffering, the
extension of human rights to everyone, the end of hierarchy and
deference, unprecedented stress on the development of all citizens,
and the end of war between Western nations. These aspirations,
evolved over 2,500 years, pioneered by remarkable leaders, tested
in the furnace of social conflict and compromise, resting on unique
religious and political concepts and on optimism about humanity's
destiny, made conceivable by the triumphs of science, technology
and automatic economic growth, came, in the last half-century,
remarkably close to fulfilment. Even coming close is an astounding
achievement.

How could we not have noticed? Where are the writers, politicians and broadcasters urging 'one last push' to achieve something
noble and immensely gratifying? Why are we fixated by potential
disasters and not by potential glory, glory defined not by blood and
empire but by universal human dignity and freedom?

Alas, the dangers are real, the foreboding is justified, and
modern society is not given to simple enthusiasm or serious
common aspiration. Our social bonds have been relaxed, our
hopes have been individualized, and our fears have been collec-
tivized. Those who think about the world as a whole are realistic to
a fault. We are mesmerized by malign forces. We have completely
given up on the idea that we can control those forces and forge a
great civilization for the benefit of everyone.

Fragmentation is triumphing, taking power from authorities
and communal institutions and empowering individuals. This
makes it more difficult to structure society for the common good.
But it does not make it impossible. True, the decisions that matter
are increasingly taken at the individual level, so society cannot

continue to thrive unless most people behave responsibly. The warning signals are evident throughout the West, with much evidence of social disintegration, compulsive consumerism, decadence and dependence, overwhelming personal egotism and retreat into the psychological twilight of purely personal, privatized worlds.

Yet, it is in the interests of every individual to continue to enjoy a society that works for everyone, and to make kindness and love central to their personal aspirations. Westerners are also powerfully conditioned by their background and culture, even today, to combine activism with compassion, self-advancement with conscience and consideration. This common heritage may be somewhat weaker than it was, but its robustness may surprise us. How else do we explain the continued cooperative behaviour of most citizens at a time when the prevailing ideology is cynical, unremitting and self-destructive selfishness? The strength of the underlying collaborative instinct can be seen in the automatic response of ordinary citizens at moments of great crisis, for example in the wake of terrorist attacks in New York, Madrid and London.

Ultimately the West rests on *one* great idea and *one* set of actions, one that stands behind and unites the six great ideas of Western civilization. The great idea, the common strand, is taking *personal responsibility* to improve oneself and the world. This was the legacy of Christianity, the idea that God is interested in every man and woman, their interior thoughts, their individuality and their actions. This idea has survived the partial disappearance of God completely intact – the soul has evolved into the self, and non-believing Westerners believe they have an interior self just as strongly as their Christian neighbours. Personal responsibility led to optimism and activism, and the other way round. Personal responsibility, and belief in a rational single benign Force in the universe, led to experimental science. Personal responsibility also stimulated a class of urban activists – merchants, international traders and explorers, free artisans, craftsmen, artists and inventors

– who used science and technology to create automatic growth. The growth of ambitious, self-confident and self-improving lower classes led, slowly over many centuries, to the idea that the community should control the state, and ultimately to democracy and a fierce commitment to equality of opportunity for everyone. The idea of personal responsibility, and the taking of it by hundreds of millions of people, has led to a degree of creative individuality in the West that has no parallel in history or in contemporary geography, either in the richness of its intellectual and practical results, or in the challenge to established ideas and authority anywhere in the world.

The West stands for personal responsibility; it stands or falls by personal responsibility. Will it stand or fall?

To be sure, hundreds of millions of Westerners, believers and non-believers, *are* taking personal responsibility for their lives, seeking to improve themselves and the world around them. The great majority of these prototypical Westerners do so quietly, unobtrusively, generally without thinking about what they are doing. They are homemakers, workers, volunteers; individuals making up their own minds about how to live their lives, taking full responsibility for their actions, acknowledging their weaknesses and their failings, but seeking to love and be loved and make the most of their personal potential.

There are, however, hundreds of millions of other Westerners, believers and non-believers, who find the modern world too confusing, too ambiguous, too threatening and simply *too difficult*. These are people who are either *victims* or *obedient followers*, or both, people who see themselves as failures, who lack self-esteem, and who may be addicted to alcohol, drugs, consumption, or work; or who decline the challenge of individuality, instead following a narrow template of ordained behaviour, and try to impose that structure on other people. Many of the latter are religious fundamentalists, and their number seems to grow every day, not just outside the West, but more dangerously inside it too.

It is not just a matter of numbers, of responsible Westerners versus those declining personal responsibility. If it were a matter of numbers, those taking responsibility might very well prevail. The many are often smarter than the few; the greatest tragedies of the twentieth century were imposed on the many by the few, who denied or bypassed democracy. The real danger today, too, comes not from ordinary people but from opinion-setters, from intellectual and anti-intellectual trends, from prevailing attitudes, from *ideas and attitudes* invented and spread by those who ought to know better, from celebrities and popular icons, from the media, from authoritarian evangelists, unscrupulous politicians, selfish business heads, and intellectuals, both ultra-liberals and neo-conservatives.

For the first time in history, we see people who have succeeded, through their own efforts, preaching not the gospel of striving and success, of optimism and the common good, but the ideology of cynicism, pessimism and the victim mentality. Having risen through the ladder of liberal society and the intellectual heritage of the West, these new elites kick away the ladder and deny the ascent to younger people.[1] Personal achievement, intellectual distinction, community loyalty, reason and truth are denigrated. Equally dangerous, we see other leaders, especially those in political power, and especially in the West's most powerful country, turning their backs on liberalism, equality, human rights and compassion for all humankind, using the excuses of terrorism, crime, immigration, asylum-seekers and 'low standards' to reassert authority at home and build empires abroad. The ultra-liberals and the neo-conservatives affect to despise each other; but they need each other and they support each other mightily. Their effect is horribly similar. The common theme is denial of internal responsibility; the one through indifference, the other through knowing what is good for us, through the assertion of *external* discipline and authority. Both lead to the destruction of our civilization, and both are helped along this path by the strength of the other.

---

1   George Walden (2000) *The New Elites: Making A Career in the Masses*, Penguin, London.

There is, of course, an alternative future – one based on recapturing the ideas and ideals that have made the West strong and successful over so many years; and one based, too, on determination by committed and responsible individuals to contribute to society and to their neighbours. We have seen this determination arise, for example, in a series of 'velvet revolutions' in Eastern Europe and elsewhere, where thousands of individuals exercised leadership and responsibility and peacefully overthrew dictatorial regimes. We have seen it in the astonishing transformation of South Africa, not just from apartheid to democracy, but also from the spectre of civil war to a stable society founded on forgiveness and tolerance. We have seen it in the decision of millions to take to the streets across Western cities to campaign for an end to global poverty, or for fair trade, environmental sustainability, or a vibrant countryside.[2] We have seen it at local levels, in small-scale neighbourhood democracy, and in a plethora of initiatives to improve community life. Most of these and many other public-spirited actions have happened outside the realm of traditional party politics, outside the sphere of institutional endeavours, and outside the framework of top-down leadership. But such actions represent nothing less than people coming together as free individuals to exercise personal responsibility. These are the best characteristics of the West, reasserting themselves in new ways. They show that there is life in the old beast yet.

---

2 Of course, such actions are not always totally altruistic, or realistic when they *are* selfless. World poverty, for example, is not going to be solved by demonstrations, rock concerts, generous giving or by any other *external* agency. The West has given $450 billion in aid to Africa since 1965, but it is only in places such as Botswana, where Africans themselves have been responsible for putting liberal institutions and sensible economic policies in place, that people have escaped poverty.

Conclusion

Christianity. Optimism. Science. Growth. Liberalism. Individualism. An interlocking set of ideas and beliefs, practices and actions, that once defined, and still define, a great civilization, one that looked both inward and outward, that aimed to liberate and lift the human soul, men and women, rich and poor, insiders and outsiders, East and West, North and South. A civilization that hoped so much, and achieved so much. A civilization that, bizarrely, has given up on ideas that have delivered so magnificently? A civilization fated to fail through self-imposed limitations? A civilization set to turn into one much less attractive, and, before long, one probably much less successful?

That which is imposed by individuals on themselves can also be removed by them. Collective suicide is quite possible. It may even be likely. But no, it is certainly not inevitable.

Western civilization has reached a fork. Down one road, the road currently bearing more traffic, lies cynicism, unmitigated self-ishness, indifference, re-centralization and aggression – attributes both advocated and practised by different elements in society, yet wholly supportive of their apparent opposites. This road could take many forms, from anarchy to neo-fascism, environmental collapse to a new American empire. All such forms, however, would mark the end of Western civilization as the democratic and individualistic ideal Europeans and Americans have imagined, nurtured and drawn closer to over hundreds of years. Western civilization will not be destroyed by our enemies; but it may be destroyed by ourselves.

Down the other road lies a recovery of nerve; confidence in our selves and our culture; emotional unity within America and within Europe, and between Europe and America, and with other European settlements; a society and civilization comprising a billion responsible individuals, bound together not by authority or coercion or unquestioned traditional beliefs, but by self-discovered and self-validated attitudes of personal striving, optimism, reason, compassion, equality, individualism and mutual identity. This road is well paved and brightly lit. Travelling it is not that hard; but it requires a change of direction.

Whether it is completed or not, the destiny of the West – springing from its unique ideas, and evident in what it has already substantially attained – is to create a fully humane, free and rich civilization, by releasing the hopes, and, more importantly, the potential and moral qualities, of all its people; and, *just conceivably, in the fullness of time*, a model attractive enough to excite most of humankind.

Index